LA CIVILTÀ CATTOLICA

LA CIVILTÀ CATTOLICA

BEATUS POPULUS, CUIUS DOMINUS DEUS EIUS

Copyright, 2017, Union of Catholic Asian News

All rights reserved. Except for any fair dealing permitted under the Hong Kong Copyright Ordinance, no part of this publication may be reproduced by any means without prior permission. Inquires should be made to the publisher.

Title: La Civiltà Cattolica, English Edition

ISSN: 2207-2446

ISBN:
    978-1-925612-06-6 (paperback)
    978-1-925612-07-3 (ebook)
    978-1-925612-08-0 (kindle)

Editor-in-chief
ANTONIO SPADARO SJ

Editorial Board
Antonio Spadaro SJ – Director
Giancarlo Pani SJ – Vice-Director
Domenico Ronchitelli SJ –Senior Editor
Giovanni Cucci SJ, Diego Fares SJ,
Francesco Occhetta SJ, Giovanni Sale SJ

Emeritus editor:
Virgilio Fantuzzi SJ,
Giandomenico Mucci SJ,
GianPaolo Salvini SJ

Published by

Union of Catholic Asian News

P.O. Box 80488, Cheung Sha Wan, Kowloon, Hong Kong

Phone: +852 2727 2018

Fax: +852 2772 7656

www.ucanews.com

Publishers: Michael Kelly SJ and Robert Barber
Production Manager: Rangsan Panpairee

CONTENTS 0317

> 15 Apr 2017
> Monthly
> Year 1

1   The Figure of the Bishop According to Pope Francis
Diego Fares, SJ

19   Women and the Diaconate
Giancarlo Pani, SJ

32   Protecting Children in the Catholic Church
Hans Zollner, SJ

42   The Border as a Bridge: Migration in Latin America and the Caribbean
Mauricio Garcian Duran, SJ - Gina Paola Sanchez Gonzalez

50   Venezuela: The Misery of King Midas
Arturo Peraza, SJ

64   Louis Lebret: The Legacy of the Mentor of *Populorum Progressio*
Fernando de la Iglesia Viguiristi S.J

78   Mysticism Without God
Giandomenico Mucci, SJ

85   The World of Almodovar
Virgilio Fantuzzi, SJ

ABSTRACTS

ARTICLE
1 THE FIGURE OF THE BISHOP
According to Pope Francis

Diego Fares, SJ

Opening the 68th General Assembly of the Italian Bishops' Conference, Pope Francis asked the bishops not to be pilots, but real pastors. On several occasions the pontiff has appealed for "shepherd bishops, not princes." With two simple gestures, as a shepherd and not a prince, Francis, when newly elected Pope, represented the great tradition of the Church and the Vatican, creating a new spiritual dynamism among the People of God. A fully pastoral image of the figure of the bishop according to Pope Francis is the image of the "shepherd with the smell of the sheep." An image capable encompassing the other figures the pope proposes: the shepherd who is close to everybody, who walks with his people, who is a man of communion.

ARTICLE
19 WOMEN AND THE DIACONATE

Giancarlo Pani, SJ

On May 12, 2016, when meeting the Superiors General of the Women's Religious Orders, Pope Francis announced a commitment to establish a commission to study the diaconate of women. This was unexpected news; however, three months later Pope Francis' announcement came into being. The early Church had a female diaconate for certain baptismal functions, a role which in the West has disappeared, but in the East has remained, albeit marginal. Today, the role of women in the family and in society has undergone radical changes. It would be peculiar if the Church were to agree with the emancipation of women in society in general, but were not to reconsider their role within the Church itself. The example of Jesus in the Gospels is emblematic; according to Paul, among standing before God there is "no longer male or female." With the guidance of the Spirit Pope Francis wants to listen to women. What are the prospects for the future?

ABSTRACTS

ARTICLE
32   PROTECTING CHILDREN IN THE CATHOLIC CHURCH

Hans Zollner, SJ

The problem of sexual abuse of minors committed by clergy is constantly returning to the forefront of media attention. There is no doubt that the protection of children and young people from sexual violence remains an issue for the Church and for society. It is also true however that the Church has become aware of the situation and is leading the way in the prevention and the protection of minors who are victims of abuse. This is recognized by non-ecclesial institutions. In this area, we look at the example of the work of the Center for Child Protection at the Pontifical Gregorian University, which promotes prevention and is dedicated to helping those countries that so far have done little to form personnel to work on these matters locally.

FOCUS
42   THE BORDER AS A BRIDGE
Migration in Latin America and the Caribbean

Mauricio Garcian Duran, SJ - Gina Paola Sanchez Gonzalez

The issue of migration is emerging as a global challenge. One location in the world that can serve as an important point of observation is Latin America and the Caribbean. For example, the border between Mexico and the US, the one between Haiti and the Dominican Republic, and the one between Venezuela and Colombia; a common occurrence is the continuously increasing freedom of movement of goods and capital, while movement of persons is increasingly and dramatically limited, a contradiction which reinforces the very causes of migratory flows. Is it time to think about boundaries as bridges, bridges that create interactions, rather than borders that separate?

ABSTRACTS

FOCUS
50   VENEZUELA: THE MISERY OF KING MIDAS

Arturo Peraza, SJ

How can a country with as much oil wealth as Venezuela, a country with an advantageous place in the American continental geography, and with such progress made during the second half of the twentieth century, need humanitarian aid, medicines and food? The country's current situation seems to be the result of an economic and political system entirely dependent on the extraction of oil, and the subsequent allocation of its income. Not even the Bolivarian revolution has gone beyond this model, and there are grave consequences for the country's democratic and social life. The only possible way forward appears to be that of the reconstruction of a social pact. The Holy See is a foremost supporter of this project.

PROFILE
64   LOUIS LEBRET
The Legacy of the Mentor of *Populorum Progressio*

Fernando de la Iglesia Viguiristi S.J.

July 20, 2016 was the fiftieth anniversary of the death of Fr. Louis Lebret. This Dominican from Brittany is not very well-known. However, we have no doubt that the grand mentor of *Populorum Progressio* deserves attention and study. Therefore, in this article we will discuss his life, thought and spirituality, providing a contribution towards recognizing the value of his legacy.

ABSTRACTS

ARTICLE
78   MYSTICISM WITHOUT GOD

Giovanni Cucci, SJ

In the light of true Christian mysticism, the article outlines the phenomenon of a different sort of mysticism, debtor to cultural and sociological factors. It is ambiguous in its ideal motivations and its practical consequences. At best, it is nothing other than a form of secular quest for meaning, something still sought even by our contemporaries.

ARTICLE
85   THE WORLD OF ALMODOVAR

Virgilio Fantuzzi, SJ

Developed from three stories by Canadian writer Alice Munro and merged into a single narrative, the film *Julieta* by Pedro Almodovar paints the portrait of a woman who is imprisoned in a sinister fate. This fate, conditioned by judgments conceived about her and the absence of benevolence is expressed enigmatically, but never uttered clearly. People interpret her actions, erroneously attributing to them her intentions. The film offers the opportunity for an excursus through the work of the Spanish director who has been making films since the 1980s. In his work, he interprets the changes of mentality which have occurred in Spain.

Now Available

LA CIVILTÀ CATTOLICA

English Edition

Annual Digital Subscription
$79

Annual Print Subscription
Asia: **$160***
Australia/NZ/Oceania: **$200***
USA/UK/Ireland/
Europe: **$220***
Rest of the world: **$260***

Print + Digital Bundle
Asia: **$200***
Australia/NZ/Oceania: **$240***
USA/UK/Ireland/
Europe: **$260***
Rest of the world: **$280***

Prices in US Dollars
* Rates include postage & handling

Educational and bulk rates are available, please email info@laciviltacattolica.com

Subscribe today at
laciviltacattolica.com

In Edition 0317:

- The Figure of the Bishop According to Pope Francis
- Women and the Diaconate
- Protecting Children in the Catholic Church
- The Border as a Bridge: Migration in Latin America and the Caribbean
- Venezuela: The Misery of King Midas
- Louis Lebret: The Legacy of the Mentor of Populorum Progressio
- Mysticism Without God
- The World of Almodovar

The Figure of the Bishop According to Pope Francis

Diego Fares, SJ

In his opening address to the 68th General Assembly of the Italian Episcopal Conference in May 2015, Pope Francis asked the bishops not to be "pilots" but real "pastors."[1] On many occasions the pontiff has appealed to bishops to be "bishops who are pastors, not princes," making references to images he had already used when he governed his previous diocese.

In 2006, while giving a retreat for the bishops of Spain, in his introductory meditation on the *Magnificat,* he spoke of "feeling ourselves to be collaborators, not owners, humble servants like Our Lady, not princes." Concluding the retreat, he said – in his meditation on the phrase "the Lord reforms us" – that, "the people desire a pastor, not a refined man who loses himself in the finer things which are in vogue."[2]

This pastoral choice does not belong exclusively to bishops, but involves every "missionary disciple," each in his own state and condition. In the apostolic exhortation, *Evangelii Gaudium* (EG), the pope states: "Clearly Jesus does not want us to be grandees who look down upon others, but men and women of the people. This is not an idea of the pope, or one pastoral option among others; they are injunctions contained in the word of God which are so clear, direct and convincing that they need no interpretations which might diminish their power to challenge us. Let us live them *sine glossa,* without commentaries."[3]

---

1. Pope Francis, *Discourse to the 68th General Assembly of the Italian Episcopal Conference*, May 18, 2015.
2. Papa Francesco/J. M. Bergoglio, *In Lui solo la speranza. Esercizi spirituali ai vescovi spagnoli* (January 15-22, 2006), Milan, Jaca Book, 2013, 14; 82.
3. Pope Francis, Apostolic exhortation *Evangelii Gaudium*, 271.

The image "pastors, not princes" is not used pejoratively, although some in the media have interpreted it as a rebuke to bishops and priests. It is something that it is much more profound. It goes back to the discernment of an epochal shift and, even more significantly, it is an invitation to ensure that no bishop, no priest allows himself to be robbed of the joy of being a pastor.[4] "By so doing we will know the missionary joy of sharing life with God's faithful people as we strive to light a fire in the heart of the world" (EG 271).

Bishops who keep watch over their people

Expressed in the very title "bishop" – in Greek, *episkopos* – there is a specific charism on which the then Cardinal Bergoglio reflected in the Synod of 2001, dedicated to "The Bishop: Servant of the Gospel of Jesus Christ for the Hope of the World." That charism, a particular mission of the bishop, consists in *keeping watch*.

It is worth reading his entire text: "The bishop is the one who *keeps watch*, he safeguards hope, keeping watch over his people (1 Pt 5:2). The spiritual attitude is the one that accents *overseeing* the flock with a view of the whole. The bishop is the one who takes care of all that keeps the flock together, a cohesive whole. Another spiritual attitude accents the need to *be vigilant* for dangers. Both attitudes have to do with the essential mission of the bishop and acquire the totality of their strength from the attitude I consider to be most essential, which consists in *keeping watch*.

"One of the most powerful images of this attitude is that found in the book of Exodus, in which we are told that Yahweh watched over his people on the night of the Passover, also known as "a night of vigil" (Ex 12:42). What I want to underline is the profound nature of keeping watch, in comparison to a watching over in a more general sense or in respect to a more pointed supervision. Overseeing refers more

---

4. From "pastoral sloth": cf. EG 83.

to the care for doctrine and customs, while keeping watch alludes more to making sure that there is salt and light in the hearts of the faithful. Being vigilant speaks of being at the ready before imminent dangers; keeping watch, instead, speaks of patiently sustaining the processes through which the Lord carries forward the salvation of his people. To be vigilant, it is sufficient to be awake, astute, quick. To keep watch requires meekness, patience and consistency of proven charity. Overseeing and being vigilant speak to us of a certain control. Instead, *keeping watch* speaks to us of hope, the hope of the merciful Father who keeps watch over the process of the hearts of his children. Keeping watch manifests and consolidates the *parresia* of the bishop, which shows Hope 'without distorting the Cross of Christ.'

"Together with the image of Yahweh who keeps watch over the great exodus of the People of the Covenant, there is another image, more familiar, but equally powerful: that of Saint Joseph. It is he who keeps watch even in his dreams over the Child and his Mother. From this profound watching over of Saint Joseph is born that silent view of the whole capable of caring for his tiny flock with impoverished means; and from it sprouts the vigilant and astute gaze which was able to avoid all of the dangers which threatened the Child."[5] The sleeping Saint Joseph, to whom Pope Francis entrusts his "slips of paper" so that "he dreams of them" is the image of the bishop, the pastor who keeps watch over his people.

Bishops who lower themselves and include others

Downward and outward, toward all. With two simple movements of a pastor and not a prince, Francis, just after being elected pope, placed himself within the great tradition of the Church and of Vatican II, generating a new spiritual dynamism in the faithful People of God.

---

5. J. M. Bergoglio, "Sorvegliare la coesione del gregge". Intervention at the Synod on "The Bishop: Servant of the Gospel of Jesus Christ for the Hope of the World", in Oss. Rom., October 4, 2001, 10. Cfr Papa Francesco/J. M. Bergoglio, *In Lui solo la speranza…*, cit., 35.

The Council tells us that as Christ "who emptied himself" and was sent "to announce the good news to the poor," so too the Church is called to follow the same path and, therefore, "encompasses with love all who are afflicted with human suffering and in the poor and afflicted sees the image of its poor and suffering Founder" (*Lumen Gentium* [LG], n.8).

When Pope Francis bowed his head to receive the blessing of his people, and every time he gets into the popemobile and rides around the entirety of Saint Peter's Square, or when he chooses borderlands for his papal visits, his movements make us feel, and not just see, the image of how a bishop can be among his people. It is not an image which seeks to subvert other bishops or popes, but rather one that asks to be seen and received with an attitude of friendship and closeness, the attitude of one who knows how to discover "the harmony of the Spirit in the diversity of charisms," just as Francis asked "his priests" – the cardinals – two days after his election.[6]

Not only his gestures, but also his doctrine expresses a lowering of self and an inclusivity that are the antithesis of a spiritual worldliness. These things are not "original statements" but rather they are what the Second Vatican Council asked for with simplicity: "Thus, the Church, although it needs human resources to carry out its mission, is not set up to seek earthly glory, but to proclaim, even by its own example, humility and self-sacrifice" (LG 8).

And even if it is true that public opinion and the media judge harshly when they see the attitude of a prince displayed by a prelate, it is also true that there is a great openness when they see any pastor – priest or bishop – who lowers himself and embraces all. The people of God senses that it is Christ who shepherds in her pastors. Saint Augustine stated as much: "Do not imagine that there will be no more good shepherds, or that we shall find them lacking, or that the Lord's mercy will not produce and establish them. Certainly, if there are good sheep there are also good shepherds; good sheep give rise to good

---

6. Cfr Pope Francis, Audience with the Cardinals, March 15, 2013.

shepherds. But all good shepherds are united in the one good shepherd; they form a unity. If only they feed the sheep, Christ is feeding the sheep. The friends of the bridegroom do not speak with their own voice, but they take great joy in listening to the bridegroom's voice."[7]

In concluding his speech to the Congregation for Bishops, in 2014, Pope Francis asked: "Where can we find such men [kerygmatic bishops, men of prayer, pastors]? It is not easy. Are there any? How should they be chosen? [...] Of course there are such men because the Lord does not abandon his Church. Maybe it is we who do not go out enough into the fields to find them. Maybe the warning of Samuel is appropriate for us, as well: "We will not sit at table before he has come here" (cf 1 Sam 16:11). It is this holy anxiety that I wish this Congregation lived."[8]

Bishops focused on the essential

What need to be the characteristics of the bishop that the pope proposes as the one whom the Lord uses to sanctify, instruct and pasture his people today? Francis reminded the bishops of the Italian Episcopal Conference (CEI) about them. The spirituality of the bishop is a return to the essential, to the personal relationship with Jesus Christ who says, "Follow me!" He makes us "pastors of a Church that is, above all else, the community of the Risen one."[9] The pope had said the same thing a few months earlier, at the meeting of the Congregation for Bishops: "There is a need to choose from among the followers of Christ witnesses to the Risen One. From here derives the essential criterion for sketching the face of the bishops we want to have."[10]

---

7. Saint Augustine, Sermon 46, XXX, in Id., *Sul sacerdozio*, Rome-Milan, *La Civiltà Cattolica*-Corriere della Sera, 2014, 168.
8. Pope Francis, Speech at the meeting with the Congregation for Bishops, February 27, 2014, in www.vatican.va.
9. ID., Speech to the 66th General Assembly of the CEI, April 14, 2014.
10. ID., Speech to the Congregation for Bishops, cit. n. 4.

Here then, are the two characteristics of the "bishop-witness" pointed out by the pope: one is that "he knows how to make everything that happened to Jesus relevant today"; and the other is that "[he is] not an isolated witness, but one together with the Church."[11] At the assembly of the CEI, the pope brings to the fore the aspect of "belonging to the Church" of "pastors of a Church that is the Body of the Lord."[12]

To better understand these characteristics, we should fix our gaze on Francis. Not because all bishops must resemble the pope in his style. Just the opposite; he prefers the diversity of charisms: "There is no such thing as a standard model of pastor for all Churches. Christ knows the singularity of the pastor that each Church needs to respond to its needs and help it realize its potential. Our challenge is entering into Christ's point of view, keeping sight of this singularity of the particular Churches."[13] Making the risen Christ relevant today requires that each one place himself in his unique and non-transferable situation and, staying himself, be faithful to the essential, harmonizing his vital witness with that of other witnesses.

To speak of the essential, it is important to consider the first time Francis spoke of the bishop. In his first *Urbi et Orbi* blessing, he mentioned "bishop" four times: referring to the conclave, he said that the duty of the conclave was to "give a bishop to Rome." Thanking the "diocesan community of Rome" for the welcome given to him, he said that it "had its bishop." He asked that the community "say a prayer for our bishop emeritus, Benedict XVI." He delineated his own mission in terms of a journey: "And now, we begin this journey: bishop and people" and he asked "the prayer of the people, asking a blessing for your bishop."[14]

The pope also mentioned the figure of the bishop in the homily of the Mass with the cardinals, describing all pastors as "disciples of Christ crucified": "When we walk without the

---

11. Ivi.
12. Id., Speech to the 66th General Assembly of the CEI, cit.
13. Id., Speech to the Congregation for Bishops, cit. n.1.
14. Id., *First Apostolic Blessing* Urbi et Orbi, March 13, 2013.

Cross, when we build without the Cross and when we confess Christ without the Cross, we are not disciples of the Lord: we are mundane, we are bishops, priests, cardinals, and popes, but not disciples of the Lord."[15] As stated in *Lumen Gentium*: "the Church 'presses forward amid the persecutions of the world and the consolations of God,' announcing the cross and death of the Lord until He comes" (cf. 1 Cor 11:26)" (LG 8; cf. LG 3; 5; 42).

Equally significant is the manner in which, in his audience with the cardinals, Pope Francis described the figure of Benedict XVI: "The petrine ministry, lived with total dedication, had in him a wise and humble interpreter, with his gaze fixed always on Christ, Risen, present and alive in the Eucharist."[16]

Lower oneself, include others and be centered: three movements around the crucified and risen Lord with which the pope invites bishops to design their own image and to see themselves as pastors of the People of God.

A bishop of Vatican II: anointed to anoint

In his first Chrism Mass as bishop of Rome, Francis considered pastors in the fundamental tension that constitutes them: ones anointed in order to anoint the faithful people of God they serve. The Council states, "that duty, which the Lord committed to the shepherds of His people, is a true service, which in sacred literature is significantly called 'diakonia' or ministry" (LG 24). "The good priest can be recognized by how his people is anointed; this is clear proof."[17] The spirit of the Second Vatican Council is concentrated in this being "for" the people, the spirit of which the pope does not say that "he should live it" but that "he is living it," together with all the bishops, priests and laity who rejoice, as missionary disciples, in going out in

---

15. ID., Homily at the Mass "*Pro Ecclesia*", March 14, 2013.
16. ID., *Audience with the Cardinals*, cit.
17. ID., *Homily at the Mass of Chrism*, March 28, 2013. Cf. Second Ecumenical Vatican Council, Decree *Christus Dominus (CD)*, nn. 12; 15; 16.

mission together with him.[18]

The relational character and dynamic of anointing animate the simple phrases of the first discourses of Pope Francis. Bishop and people take a journey together in which "the entire body of the faithful, anointed as they are by the Holy One, (cf Jn 2:20, 27) cannot err in matters of belief. They manifest this special property by means of the whole people's supernatural discernment in matters of faith when 'from the Bishops down to the last of the lay faithful' they show universal agreement in matters of faith and morals" (LG 12).

This journey made together is "synod" and in that word breathes the synodal spirit of Vatican II: "From the very first centuries of the Church, bishops...pooled their abilities and their wills for the common good and for the welfare of the individual Churches. Thus came into being synods, provincial councils and plenary councils... This sacred ecumenical Council earnestly desires that the venerable institution of synods and councils flourish with fresh vigor" (CD 36).

Regarding the continuity between Pope Francis and Pope Benedict XVI, here is an example in the words that Benedict spoke to the Argentine bishops in 2009, when he spoke of the "holy oil of priestly anointing," that makes the pastor like Christ "in the midst of the People." On that occasion, Pope Benedict reminded the bishops and the priests that each of them must "always behave among his faithful as one who serves (cf. LG 27)" without seeking honor, caring for the "People of God" with "tenderness and mercy."[19] This same image of the bishop that Pope Benedict presented to the Argentine bishops, Pope Francis is proposing to all bishops, in order that they live it fully, in this moment in history.

The pastoral image of the bishop

18. "Moreover, the care of souls should always be infused with a missionary spirit so that it reaches out as it should to everyone living within the parish boundaries" *(CD 30).*

19. Benedict XVI, *Address to the bishops of the Argentine Episcopal Conference during their* "ad limina" *visit*, April 30, 2009, n. 2.

It is possible to focus the image of the bishop according to Pope Francis in a totally pastoral milieu, that of the "pastor with the smell of his sheep." But we should not take this just as some original way of speaking but rather as an image capable of unifying in itself all of the other images the pope proposes. The image of the pastor with the smell of his sheep on him and with the smile of a father[20] attracts and draws together other images into a constellation, as if it were one great "star-pastor."

In what sense is this pastoral prospective the key to the figure of the bishop? Bergoglio said in 2009: "In the language of the Council and Aparecida, 'pastoral' is not opposed to 'doctrinal' but rather, includes it. The pastoral is not a mere 'practical, contingent application of theology.' Quite the opposite, Revelation itself, and all of theology, is pastoral, in the sense that it is the Word of salvation, the Word of God for the life of the world. As Crispino Valenziano said, 'It is not the case that one needs to adapt the pastoral to doctrine but that it is necessary to not rip away the original and constitutive pastoral seal from doctrine. The 'anthropological route' that is followed in theology without doubt or perplexity is that which runs parallel to a 'pastoral' doctrine: we men receive revelation and salvation perceiving the knowledge that God has of our nature and his lowering of himself as pastor toward each of his sheep."[21]

Bergoglio continues: "This integrated conception of doctrine and pastoral (that led the documents with permanent doctrine to be called 'Constitution' – not only the dogmatic *Lumen Gentium*, but also the pastoral *Gaudium et Spes*) is clearly reflected in the Decree on priestly formation. The Decree insists on the importance of forming pastors of souls, shepherds who,

---

20. Pope Francis, *Homily during the Chrism Mass*, April 2, 2015. Pope John Paul II used a similar expression: "I think of the reassuring smile of Pope Luciani, that in the brief span of a month conquered the world" (John Paul II, s. *Homily* of September 27, 2003).

21. C. Valenziano, *Vegliando sul gregge*, Magnano (Bi), Qiqajon, 1994, 16, cited in J. M. Bergoglio, *Significado e importancia de la formacion academica. Reunion Plenaria de la Pontificia Comision para America Latina*, February 18, 2009.

united to the one Good and Beautiful Shepherd (beautiful in as much as he leads by attraction and not by imposition), 'feeds his sheep' (Cf. Jn 21:15-17)."[22] In fact, "the image of the Good Shepherd is the *analogatum princeps* of all formation. When they speak of the pastoral end as the ultimate end, both Vatican II and Aparecida intend 'pastoral' in the inclusive sense: not in as much as it is distinguished from other aspects of formation but in that it includes them all. It includes them in the love of the Good Shepherd, given that love 'is the form of all virtues,' as Saint Thomas Aquinas says, following Saint Ambrose."[23]

When Pope Francis speaks of the triple mission of the Church and of the bishops, he picks up the thought of Benedict XVI, who presented the triple *munus* of the pastor in new accents: "The Church's deepest nature is expressed in her three-fold responsibility: of proclaiming the word of God (*kerygma-martyria*), celebrating the sacraments (*leitourgia*), and exercising the ministry of charity (*diakonia*). These duties presuppose each other and are inseparable."[24] Note that when he speaks of teaching, Benedict XVI uses the expression *kerygma-martyria*, the same that Francis uses when he wishes for kerygmatic bishops and witness of the Risen One.

When he speaks of the mission of guiding, Benedict uses the term *diakonia*, service in love, that Francis also puts first.[25] This aspect of *diakonia* is no less essential than the other two components. Benedict writes: "For the Church, charity is not a kind of welfare activity which could equally well be left to others, but is a part of her nature, an indispensable expression of her very being."[26] The discernment of Benedict XVI in writing his encyclicals consisted in comprehending that the world

22. Ivi.

23. Ivi. The text of Thomas cited in the original is, "*Ambrosius dicit, quod caritas est forma et mater virtutum*" (Aquinas, s., *De virtutibus*, 2, 3, *sed contra*).

24. Benedict XVI, Encyclical *Deus Caritas est* (December 25, 2005), n. 25. Cf, CD 11 and 30; LG 7.

25. "By her very nature the Church is missionary; she abounds in effective charity and a compassion which understands, assists and promotes" (EG, 179).

26. Benedict XVI, Encyclical *Deus Caritas est*, cit., n. 25.

needed to be spoken to of love. And love has "the smell of the sheep."

Pastors with the smell of their sheep and the smile of a father

Pope Francis has no difficulty speaking about the "sins of pastors" – including his own and those of the Curia – to a world like ours in which the "sense of sin" is diminished.[27] Nevertheless, his most emblematic phrase regarding pastors, the one which has touched everyone's heart, does not regard the restrictive ethical, but the irresistibly attractive aesthetical. The famous phrase is: I want "pastors with the smell of sheep on them" and "the smile of a father," as he added last Holy Thursday. This is the image of the bishop that Francis holds in his heart. It is the same for priests, for cardinals and for the pope himself; shepherds who do not want to merely dress themselves in sheep's wool but who are passionate about serving them.[28]

We can note here that, more than the image of a bishop, we are speaking about an odor. An odor that, like all strong odors, clearly evokes many images. But the principal one is that which is to be read *sine glossa*,[29] that which is to be smelled, it is that of shepherds who care for their sheep and not for themselves.

Together with the image of the "pastor with the smell of his sheep," the parable of the Good Shepherd, so often heard but so infrequently lived out, imposes itself with the strength of a fresh breeze that wakes us from ideological daydreams and our routine, putting us back on our journey with evangelical passion. The shepherd saturates himself with the smell of his sheep when he is among his people. It is not possible to create this smell in a laboratory. And the pastor does not become infected with it when he is around his people, grazing: it is his own odor of himself as a sheep, and it reminds him that the people he shepherds are the people he himself was called from.

"The smell of the sheep" unites the Bergoglian themes

---

27. Pope Francis, *Homily*, January 31, 2014.
28. Cf. D. Fares, "*Pasci il mio gregge*", in Agostino, s., *Sul sacerdozio*, cit., VI.
29. EG 271.

of anointing,[30] of keeping watch and of keeping safe, of discernment, ready to feed the flock with sound doctrine and to defend it from enemies, that is from wolves who, though dressed as sheep, cannot hide their "smell of wolves." In this way, the spiritual sense of smell allows the bishop to uncover and reject the temptation to a spiritual worldliness, with its sophisticated perfumes, giving him an "olfactive" criterion for discernment, so that he remains within the flock from which he was drawn and is recognized by the sheep, in a way so as not to lose them.

Bishops who pray with their people

In the thought of Pope Francis, the personal prayer and liturgical prayer of the pastor, like his anointing, are not something destined to perfume his own person; rather, they should "spread out and reach the periphery," like the oil that drips from Aaron's beard, down to the fringes of his garments.[31]

Therefore, the prayer of the pastor, to which the pope makes reference, is always filled with faces; and "our exhaustion" is "like incense that rises silently to heaven [...] going directly to the heart of the Father"[32] and, picking up again the image used by Francis in the most recent Chrism Mass, feels like God's caress to priests.

The image of the bishop who prays can be sketched by looking at how he is centered in Christ, spending himself in the service of his people.[33] This gives shape to his openness to God, his holiness, his personal prayer: "he ought to have the same *hypomone* and *parresia* in his prayer, which he has to exercise in

---

30. Cfr. Pope Francis, *Homily during the Chrism Mass*, March 28, 2013.

31. "Priests who perform their duties sincerely and indefatigably in the Spirit of Christ arrive at holiness by this very fact" (Vatican II, Decree *Presbyterorum Ordinis*, 13).

32. Pope Francis, *Homily during the Chrism Mass*, April 2, 2015. Cf. CD 27.

33. "Only if centered on God can one go to the peripheries of the world!" (Pope Francis, *Homily in the Church of the Gesu*, January 3, 2014. In this homily the Pope used the example of St. Peter Favre, and his desire to "let Christ occupy the center of the heart" (Cf. P. Favre, *Memorie spirituali*, Roma-Milano, La Civilta Cattolica - Corriera della Sera, 2014, 68).

preaching the Word."[34]

This is the spirituality that unleashes the concrete pastoral action that John Paul II twelve years previously urged pastors to have in the exhortation, *Pastores dabo vobis*.[35] He had already traced it out in his homily on "The spirituality of the diocesan priest today." He reminded priests of "their pastoral reason for being": "A priest (and even more so a bishop) who is not inserted into some kind of ecclesial community could certainly not present himself as a valid model of ministerial life, since this is essentially inserted in the concrete context of the interpersonal relationships of the same community."[36]

In *Pastores dabo vobis*, John Paul II presents as an exemplary figure the bishop Saint Charles Borromeo, who loved the spirituality of the Spiritual Exercises of Saint Ignatius. The Exercises propose to pastors the need to unite the contemplative and the active in the manner in which Saint Peter Favre intended: "The one who seeks God spiritually in good works will better find him in prayer, than if he had abstained from those good works."[37] To people of the active life, the saint made this recommendation: "It will be better, all in all, that you order your prayers toward the treasure of good works rather than the opposite."[38] That is to say, one needs to look at what needs to be done and at the people with whom one must relate, and then pray asking for the grace necessary to do one's tasks as the Lord wills.

Saint Charles Borromeo wrote: "My brothers, do not forget that there is nothing so necessary to all churchmen than the meditation which precedes, accompanies and follows all our actions: I will sing, says the prophet, and I will meditate (cf. Ps. 100:1). If you administer the sacraments, my brother, meditate upon what you are doing. If you celebrate Mass, meditate on what you are offering. If you recite the psalms in choir, meditate to whom and of what you are speaking. If you are guiding souls,

---

34. Pope Francis, *Speech to the Congregation for Bishops*, cit. n. 7.
35. John Paul II s., Apostolic Exhortation *Pastores dabo vobis*, March 25, 1992.
36. Id., *Homily* of November 4, 1980.
37. Cf. P. Favre, *Memorie spirituali*, cit. nn.126-127.
38. Ivi.

meditate in whose blood they have been cleansed. And let all be done among you in charity (1 Cor. 16:14)."[39]

Therefore, the transcendence of which Pope Francis constantly speaks is double: toward God and his saints, in prayer; toward the neighbor, toward the people of God. As he said to the Mexican bishops: "do not forget prayer. It is a bishop's "negotiation" with God on behalf of his people. Do not forget it! And the second transcendence is closeness to one's people."[40]

So, the odor of the sheep is not only the smell of the earthly sheep, but also of those who are already in the heavenly pastures: it is the pleasant aroma of the saintly sheep, that can be acquired by frequenting them in prayer and in the reading of their lives. In the image of the bishop that the pope has in mind, the example of the saints – and in particular those who were great evangelizers of peoples – is essential. The saints that the pope is canonizing with the so-called "equivalent methodology" are figures that have realized a "great evangelization and are in harmony with the spirituality and the theology of *Evangelii Gaudium*. For this reason, I have chosen these examples."[41] They are women and men, evangelizers loved by their people who inculturated themselves in order to inculturate the Gospel.

This desire to inculturate the Gospel exercised a strong influence on the prayer of the bishop evangelizer and pastor. Bergoglio has always been a bishop who prayed to the saints together with his people, having been inclined to popular piety since his youth, thanks to his grandmother Rosa, who "told him the stories of the saints" and "accompanied him to processions."[42]

The image of the transcendence toward God in prayer, that the pope proposes to bishops, has much in common with the mode of

---

39. John Paul II, s., *Pastores dabo vobis*, cit. n. 72. Cf Charles Borromeo, s., *Acta Ecclesiae Mediolanensis*, Milan, 1559, 1178.

40. Pope Francis, *Speech to the bishops of the Mexican Episcopal Conference on their 'ad limina' visit*, May 19, 2014.

41. Pope Francis, *Encounter with journalists on the flight to Manila*, January 15, 2015.

42. "Since early childhood I participated in popular piety" (J. Camara – S. PFaffen, *Aquel Francisco*, Cordoba, Raiz de Dos, 2014, 31 f).

praying and adoring God proper to his faithful people. The pope wants bishops who pray with their people, bishops whose prayer is perfumed with spiritualty and with popular mysticism.

Bishops with "Christological odor"

The image of the pastor with the smell of the sheep is an emblematic one. It is one of those images that Guardini describes as "primordial" or of great evocative power.[43] Even if it has been cited and utilized to the point of becoming a stereotype, it can still provide the starting point for a brief theoretical reflection. This is only a draft, an invitation to enter into the theological, anthropological and ontologically dense language of Pope Francis.

First of all, it is necessary to give the proper weight to the metaphor used by the pontiff. There are some people who do not understand this language: it seems to them to be rough, not fit for a pope and even without theological content. This fact is truly singular and gives rise to this thought: the people "understand him," while the intellectuals "don't appreciate him." Some think that this desire of touching the hearts of the people is nothing more than popularism. Is it? Not at all. Well illumined faith is not only for the educated. It is an illumination that comes from the anointing of the Holy Spirit and it is that which is given to the humble making them wiser than the wise of our culture (cf. Mt 11:25-27; 1 Jn 2:26-27).

The pope's metaphors should be appreciated for what they are: images that in the sea of words of today's world act like the shepherd's whistle. His sheep know it well and let themselves be guided by it. The language of Pope Francis is not only "original" – the language of a Latin American – but, being clear, it is also

true and does the heart good. As Aristotle said, being capable of

---

43. R. Guardini, *L'opera d'arte*, Brescia, Morcelliana, 1998, 21.

using metaphors is a sign of a higher intelligence.[44]

If we contemplate the image of the pastor with the odor of his sheep from a Trinitarian perspective and we liberally follow the custom of the Church Fathers, who like Saint Augustine, attributed a quality to one of the Divine Persons, we could say that the odor of the sheep is proper to the Person of Christ. It is a Christological odor, the odor of the incarnation and of the passion, of bandages and blood. It is the sweat of the one who walks with his disciples and who sees around him the crowds; it is the odor of the washing of the feet and the odor of the bandages of a stinking Lazarus; it is also a feminine perfume, like that of Mary, that fills the home; the aroma of lilies of the field and of wind and water toward which Christ commands Peter to row.

John Paul II affirmed: "The Christological dimension of the pastoral ministry, considered in depth, leads to an understanding of the Trinitarian foundation of ministry itself. Christ's life is Trinitarian. He is the eternal and only-begotten Son of the Father and the anointed of the Holy Spirit, sent into the world; it is he who, together with the Father, pours out the Spirit upon the Church. This Trinitarian dimension, manifested in every aspect of Christ's life and activity, also shapes the life and activity of the bishop. Rightly, then, the Synod Fathers chose explicitly to describe the life and ministry of the bishop in the light of the Trinitarian ecclesiology contained in the teaching of the Second Vatican Council."[45]

This Christological odor illumines the anthropology of Pope Francis and it makes us think of his choice to take as his starting point the beautiful, before the true and the good. It is a discernment of his which the ears of the sheep need to hear today, saturated as we are by discussions of dogmatic definitions and impractical moral advice.

With the beautiful, the *pulchrum*, the good also enters, and

---

44. Aristotle, *Poetica*, 1459a 5f. Aristotle affirmed that creating metaphors is an "incommunicable gift" and yet all can appreciate them.
45. John Paul II, s., Apostolic Exhortation *Pastores gregis*, (October 16, 2003), n.7.

then each one sincerely desires the truth. This is the pedagogy of the pastor. If it is thought about in philosophical terms, the odor of the sheep has to do with the *pulchrum*, a clearly Christological *pulchrum*, in that beauty and glory manifest themselves under a different form, without exaggerating, given that for the pastor the odor of his sheep is not unpleasant.

And if we look at things from a political perspective, keeping in mind the four principles of Francis, we can say that the olfactive image of the odor of the sheep corresponds to the highest principle: the odor of the sheep is "the odor of anointing," that indicates the totality of the faithful people of God, "holy and infallible *in credendo*" (EG 119). If anything is typical of a strong odor it is that it is pungent and provokes either a total rejection, like when food has rotted, or a strong attraction, like a pleasant perfume.

This odor is experienced "in the *closeness of the Pastor*": close to all, but in a special way to the sick, to the poorest and those who are far away, the excluded and the marginalized. There are two principles that are established only in closeness: that of unity, which is superior to conflict (because the very nature of conflict is to separate and contrast) and that of reality, which is superior to the ideal, because it is experienced only emerging in oneself in reality, touching open wounds and allowing oneself to become involved with one's neighbors.

If we consider the sweat of the shepherd who walks with his sheep, the image of a Church going out, that is "the paradigm of every work of the Church" (EG 15; 17; 20), then what comes to mind is the principle that time is superior to space, because the road is traced and walked upon without allowing oneself to be blocked by contrasts and without taking over spaces. As *Evangelii Gaudium* says, "Giving priority to time means being concerned about initiating processes rather than possessing spaces" (EG 223).

Men of communion and not "bishop-pilots"

The pontiff does not give lessons as to how a bishop ought to be: when he speaks of pastors, we note that he has one ear that is attentive to the Gospel and the other to the faithful (cf. EG 154). Through his words, his pauses, his examples, his smiles and his gestures, we are able to form a strong, united image of what a pastor is: centered in the love of Jesus and uniting his people, he is a man of communion.

This was the central theme of the speech to the Italian bishops in May, 2014. On that occasion, Francis made a significant gesture: he gifted the bishops the words Paul VI had spoken to the same Conference on April 14, 1964, calling for "a strong and renewed spirit of unity" that provokes a "unifying animation in spirit and in works."[46] This union is the key that the world might believe and so that they can be "Pastors of a Church […] anticipation and promise of the Kingdom," that goes out toward the world with "the eloquence of gestures" of "truth and mercy."[47]

This image of "men of communion" giving hope to the world is the last that we will indicate as the image of the bishop that is presented to us by him who today is the bishop of Rome, the Church which "presides in charity over all of the Churches."[48]

As the pontiff said to the Italian bishops on May 18, 2015, being men of communion requires a special "ecclesial sensitivity." Union is the work of the Spirit who acts thanks to bishop-pastors, not bishop-pilots. They reinforce "the indispensable role of the laity disposed to take on the responsibilities that are properly theirs." Their ecclesial sensitivity "is revealed concretely in collegiality and in the communion between bishops and their priests: in the communion among bishops: between dioceses materially and vocationally rich, and those in difficulty; between the peripheries and the center; between bishops' conferences and bishops with the successor of Peter."[49]

---

46. Pope Francis, *Speech to the 66th General Assembly of the Italian Bishops' Conference*, cit.
47. Ivi.
48. Id., *First Apostolic blessing, Urbi et orbi*, cit.
49. Id., *Speech to the 68th General Assembly of the Italian Bishops' Conference*, cit.

Women and the Diaconate

Giancarlo Pani, SJ

On May 12, 2016, at a meeting of the International Union of the Superiors General of Women's Religious Orders, one sister asked Pope Francis why women were excluded from decision-making processes in the Church and from preaching at Eucharistic celebrations. In asking, she cited his words, "the feminine genius is needed in all expressions of the life of the Church and Society."[1]

In reply, Francis mentioned the presence of women deacons in the ancient Church: "it seems that the role of the deaconesses was to help with the baptism of women, with their immersion [...] and they also anointed female bodies."

In addition, they had another task: "when there was a judgment to be made on a marriage because a husband had beaten his wife, and had gone to the bishop to report it, deaconesses were responsible for inspecting the bruises on the woman's body resulting from her husband's blows, and then informing the bishop."

The pope continued: "I would like to constitute an official commission to study the question: I think it will be good for the Church to clarify this point; I agree, and I will speak [to the Congregation] in order to do something of this nature."[2]

Three months later, on August 2, the pope honored that commitment and instituted a commission to study the theme of women's diaconate, especially from a historical perspective. The

---

1. Question from a religious sister, in Francis, *Speech to the International Union of Superiors General (IUSG)*, May 12, 2016, in vatican.va/ Cfr ID., Apostolic exhortation *Evangelii Gaudium* (November 24, 2013), n. 103.
2. Id., *Speech to IUSG*, cit.

commission has already begun its work. While awaiting the commission's conclusions, here are some historical reflections.

The Gospels and women

The Catholic and non-Catholic media spread the news of this around the world, provoking diverse and contrasting reactions. There are those who believe that the permanent diaconate of women is a return to what existed in the early Church and hence legitimate. Others see it as the first step toward the priesthood of women, and maintain that this is impossible in the Catholic Church.

The Gospels offer a new and positive stance toward women, free of prejudice: Jesus speaks in public with women, a behavior then considered improper for a teacher. He "opposes all the men who in the name of the Hebrew law wanted to condemn the adulteress; he defends the affectionate actions of Mary of Bethany; he praises the stance of love in the repentant woman as far beyond that of Simon the Pharisee; at the time of the Resurrection he shows himself first to Mary Magdalen and then to the Apostles."[3] This last choice is the most significant: it is to Mary Magdalen that the Lord entrusted the first message of the resurrection, on which Christianity is based, and her witness has spread through the entire world by evangelic proclamation.[4]

Jesus knew all too well that the testimony of women would have been received as "nonsense" (see Luke 24:11), but he chose them all the same for a primordial task of witness in the Church and to enlighten the apostles themselves.[5] Analogously, the first Christian community has an innovative way of relating to women, so much so that this period is considered by academics as a "springtime for women's ministry. [...] Many historians are convinced that, at the

    3. J. Galot, "L'accesso della donna ai ministeri della Chiesa", in *Civ. Catt.* 1972 II 325. Last year the memorial of Mary Magdalen was elevated to the level of a feast at the wish of Pope Francis. The decree, with the significant name *Apostolorum Apostola*, is dated June 3, 2016. The title "apostle of the apostles" goes back to Hippolytus of Rome.
    4. Cfr M. Perroni - C. Simonelli, *Maria di Magdala. Una genealogia apostolica*, Ariccia (Rm), Aracne, 2016, 81-117.
    5. Cfr A. Destro - M. Pesce, *Dentro e fuori le case. Il ruolo delle donne da Gesu alle prime Chiese*, Bologna, EDB, 2016, 19-30.

time of the first evangelization, women not only participated in the mission, but also directed domestic churches."[6]

Women deacons in the apostolic and sub-apostolic age

As for women deacons, there are some passages in the New Testament where they are mentioned. The Letter to the Romans speaks of them in its final chapter, where Paul writes "I commend to you Phoebe, our sister, who is also a deacon of the Church at Cenchreae" (Rm 16:1). Phoebe is the only woman deacon of the first century Church whose name is known.[7] In the text "deacon of the Church" the word for "deacon" has a feminine form,[8] and the very structure of the phrase ennobles her diaconal function without specifying her area of service. Paul also gives her another qualification, *prostatis* (one who takes care of, a benefactor), to indicate another specific role.[9]

Anyhow, it is hard not to give the term "deacon" the same meaning as "deacon of the gospel" that Paul attributes to himself and to his collaborators.[10] Origen commented on this passage: "Women were also constituted into the Church's ministry. [...] So [the apostle] teaches [...] that in the Church there are women in ministry; and those women should be assumed into the ministry who have assisted many and have merited by their good services to attain the praise of an apostle."[11]

---

6. E. Cattaneo, *I ministeri nella Chiesa antica. Testi patristici dei primi tre secoli*. Milan, Paoline, 2012, 182. See also "Il ministero delle diaconesse", in International Theological Commission, "Il diaconato: evoluzione e prospettive", in *Nuovo Enchiridion sul diaconato. Le fonti e i documenti ufficiali della Chiesa*, ed E. Petrolino, Vatican City, Libr. Ed. Vaticana, 2016, 550-557.

7. Cfr K. Madigan - C. Osiek, *Ordained Women in the Early Church*, Baltimore - London, Johns Hopkins University Press, 2005, 12f.

8. *Ousan diakonon*: a female deacon, for the community had not yet started to use the term "deaconess," which arises for the first time in the fourth century.

9. Cfr M. Scimmi, *Le antiche diaconesse nella storiografia del XX secolo. Problemi di metodo*, Milan, Glossa, 2004, 166-171.

10. Cfr *1 Cor* 3:5; *2 Cor* 3:6; 6:4; 11:15.23; *1 Ts* 3:2. See C. Marucci, "Il 'Diaconato' di Febe (*Rom* 16,1-2) secondo l'esegesi moderna", in *Diakonia, Diaconiae, Diaconato. Semantica e storia nei Padri della Chiesa. XXXVIII incontro di studiosi dell'antichità cristiana*, Rome, Augustinianum, 2010, 684-696, particularly 689.

11. Origen, *Commentary on the Letter to the Romans*, vol. II, Rome, Citta Nuova, 2016, 549.

Women also carried out functions of apostolate and prophecy as we see in Rm 16:7, "Greet Andronicus and Junia, my companions who were in prison with me; they are prominent among the apostles, *en tois apostolois.*" They are perhaps a married couple; in the Greek text, the gender of Junia is an issue, as it could be male,[12] but is in fact female.[13] St. John Chrysostom commented: "Being among the apostles is a great thing already, but being prominent among them is a great praise. [...] This woman is considered worthy of this appellative of the apostles."[14] According to Chrysostom, Junia is the name of a woman, and she is qualified with the title of the "apostles." This is the same term that Paul uses of himself in opening his Letters.[15]

Another document is the passage of *1 Tim* 3:11 where the author, after giving instructions to bishops and deacons, refers to women who must be "serious, not slanderers, but temperate, faithful in all things." But who are these *women*? Are they the wives of the deacons just mentioned? If such were so we should have expected a "their" women. The opinion of exegetes today is unanimous: these are the women deacons of the community.[16] This passage is considered an important argument for the institution of "women deacons."[17]

Here we should signal a letter of Pliny the Younger to the Emperor Trajan, which speaks of *ministrae*, a term that could be

12. However, the male name is not attested in Greek in any literary or epigraphic source.

13. This interpretation has prevailed in the Latin *Vulgate* and in history. Cfr R. Penna, *La Lettera ai Romani*, Bologna, EDB, 2010, 1084f.

14. Ivi, 1086 (PG 60, 669-670).

15. Cfr *Rm* 1:1; *Gal* 1:1; *1 Cor* 1:1 etc. See also P. A. Gramaglia, *Le diaconesse*, Turin, Tipografia Saviglianense, 2009, 216-236.

16. Cfr C. Marucci, "Storia e valore del diaconato femminile nella Chiesa antica", in *Rassegna di Teologia* 38 (1997) 771-795, particularly 772f. Note that *diakonos* in the male form (cfr *Phil* 1:1; *1 Tm* 3:8.12) is considered a written proof of diaconate, but when in the female form it is considered a problem, or at least there is a tendency to give a wider interpretation, see for example the Italian Episcopal Conference's version in 2008 of *Rm* 16:1, that translates the noun form *ousan diakonon* with a verbal form: "Phoebe, who serves the Church of Cenchreae."

17. Cfr C. Simonelli– M. Scimmi, *Donne diacono? La posta in gioco*, Padova, Messaggero, 2016, 84-89.

the translation of *diakonoi*.[18] The governor reported some news from the Christians themselves: "I thought it necessary to put to torture two slaves who were called *ministrae*."[19] While it is impossible to be precise about the functions the term alludes to, it is clear that it offers witness to the existence of a form of female diaconate in the second century.[20]

It should be noted here that in the first two centuries the terms "deacon" and "bishop" do not have a particular signification, such as that following an ordination, but indicate a commission, given by Church authority, to one Christian to carry out a particular task in the community. It is not possible to project onto these terms a meaning that is based on later sacramental interpretation.[21]

The following centuries

In the early years of the Church's history, women did not maintain such a role due to the probable reabsorption by the Judaic tradition. The passage in *1 Cor* 14:33b-35 where women are told to be silent in the assembly could well be a sign of that influence. While exegetes consider it a later addition the restriction expressed here is confirmed in *1 Tim* 2:11-12 where women are categorically forbidden "to teach or have dominion over men."

However, in the third century, women deacons were attested both by Clement of Alexandria[22] and – as we have seen – by Origen, but we cannot deduce from this that there was an *order* of deaconesses at that time. Such was documented by the *Didascalia Apostolorum* (preserved in a Syriac translation of 240). According to the liturgist Martimort, this is a text that "presents

---

18. Analogously, in the latin *Vulgate*, *ministrare* translates *diakoneo* (cfr *Mt* 20:28; *Lk* 10:40 etc.).

19. Pliny the Younger, *Lettera* 10, 96,8. Cfr C. Simonelli – M. Scimmi, *Donne diacono?...*, cit., 55-57.

20. Cfr M. Scimmi, *Le antiche diaconesse...*, cit., 173 s.

21. Cfr K. Madigan - C. Osiek, *Ordained Women...*, cit., 5.

22. Cfr Clement of Alexandria, *Stromata* III, 6, 53,4. Although Clement refers to the time of Paul.

the deaconess as a true ministry, both pastoral and liturgical."[23] Here, it refers to the baptism of women carried out through immersion; deaconesses were also carrying out baptismal unction and the task of religious education of neophytes; they also had to take care of the infirm. Nevertheless, their ministry still appeared limited: they could neither baptize nor teach.[24]

In the fourth century, Epiphanius and the *Apostolic Constitutions* make reference to the ministry of deaconesses. Epiphanius confirms that in the Church there is an "order of deaconesses"[25] whose task is to assist women during baptismal immersion and in cases of sickness. Epiphanius enters into a polemic with the priestesses of the Montanists who were censured because they were carrying out priestly functions, and recalls Scripture, noting how in the Old and New Testaments the existence of any type of female priesthood is excluded; he repeats, moreover, that there were no women among the apostles and that Mary, the mother of Jesus, did not have priesthood.[26]

At the end of the fourth century, the *Apostolic Constitutions* gave indications concerning the female functions that the deaconesses carried out in the baptismal rite, confirming those indicated by Epiphanius and adding that women were not allowed to teach or baptize, for they were precluded from the priesthood.[27]

---

23. A. G. Martimort, *Les diaconesses. Essai historique*, Rome, Centro Liturgico Vincenziano, 1982, 73-80.

24. Cfr E. Cattaneo, *I ministeri nella Chiesa antica...*, cit., 193; A. Borras - B. Pottier, *La grazia del diaconato. Questioni attuali a proposito del diaconato latino*, Assisi (Pg), Cittadella, 165-206.

25. Epiphanius, *Panarion* 79,3: but the deaconesses do not have sacerdotal offices or directive functions. Cfr P. Sorci, "Ministeri liturgici della donna nella chiesa antica", in C. Militello (ed.), *Donna e ministero*, Roma, Dehoniane, 1991, 17-96, particularly 57-60.

26. Cfr A. Piola, *Donna e sacerdozio. Indagine storico-teologica degli aspetti antropologici dell'ordinazione delle donne*, Cantalupa (To), Effatà, 2006, 129-131.

27. The *Apostolic Constitutions* came to life in the Syrian sphere and follow the text of the *Didascalia Apostolorum*. Priesthood is precluded by the Pauline injunction: "If the man is the head of the woman, it is not right that the rest of the body – in this case the woman – should command the head" (*Cost*. VIII, 1; cfr *1 Cor* 11:3).

In the rite of benediction of the deaconesses, the word "ordination," the expression "imposition of the hands," and the prayers are the same as those used for the sub-deacon and the reader.

In the West it is a text of *Ambrosiaster*, at the end of the fourth century, that affirms forcefully that only man is the image of God and so it would be a disgrace if women were to speak in the Church, as also it would be inconceivable that women be ordained to the diaconate.[28] Some particular Councils also pronounce against women who take on sacramental functions.[29] Even so, the Latin Church does have an *Oratio ad diaconam faciendam* in the *Hadrianum* sacramentary from the end of the eighth century.[30] Generally, it can be affirmed that the female diaconate was found sparingly in the West.

From the fourth to the fifth centuries, and thereafter, new factors occur: adult baptisms diminish, the type of life lived by deaconesses becomes more like that of a woman who guides the monastic communities. The deaconess, the Cappadocian Fathers attest, is now in charge of a female *coenobium* and takes care of the poor and the needy.[31] Chrysostom has an extensive epistolary exchange with various deaconesses, including with Olympia, *hegoumena* (abbess) of a monastery. Canon 15 of the Council of Chalcedon in 451 affirms that the deaconesses are ordained with the imposition of hands (*cheirotonia*); the ministry is called *leitourgia*; and that deaconesses are not allowed to marry after ordination.[32]

In the East, at least for the Byzantine period, deaconesses were ordained in women's convents. Still today the orthodox Churches have *ordained deaconesses*, an institution that has never been abolished.[33]

---

28. Cfr Ambrosiaster, *In 1 Cor* 14:34: CSEL 81/2, 163f; *Ad Tim* 3,11: CSEL 81/3, 268.
29. For example, the particular Council of Saragossa in 380, that of Nimes of 394 or 396, the 1st of Orange of 441 etc.
30. Cfr International Theological Commission, "Il diaconato…", cit., 564.
31. Cfr the witness of Basil of Caesarea and Gregory of Nyssa, in I. Trabace, "La figura della diaconessa negli scritti dei Padri Cappadoci", in *Diakonia…*, cit., 639-651.
32. Cfr International Theological Commission, "Il diaconato…", cit., 555.
33. Cfr A. Borras - B. Pottier, *La grazia del diaconato…*, cit., 175f.

The problem of the female diaconate

At Pentecost in 1994, with the apostolic letter *Ordinatio sacerdotalis*, Pope John Paul II summarized what had been developed in previous magisterial interventions (including *Inter Insigniores*), concluding that Jesus had chosen men alone for priestly ministry. So "the Church has no authority whatsoever to confer priestly ordination on women. [...] This judgment is to be definitively held by all the Church's faithful."[34] The pronouncement was a clear word for all those who maintained that the refusal of priestly ordination to women could still be discussed. Nevertheless, it permitted an idea from Paul VI to re-emerge, where he affirmed that the Church must "recognize and promote the role of women in the evangelizing mission and in the life of the Christian communities."[35]

Later, following problems raised not so much by doctrine as by the strength with which it was presented, the Congregation for the Doctrine of the Faith was asked a *quaestio*: is *Ordinatio sacerdotalis* to be "considered as belonging to the deposit of the faith?" The response was "affirmative," and the doctrine was qualified as *infallibiliter proposita*, that is "it has to be held always and everywhere by all the faithful."[36]

Difficulties in the reception of this response created tension in the relations between the Magisterium and Theology for associated problems. These are pertinent to fundamental theology concerning infallibility. It was the first time in history that the Congregation appealed explicitly to the constitution *Lumen Gentium*, n.25, where a doctrine is proclaimed infallible because it is taught as being necessary to be believed definitively by the bishops throughout the world in communion between themselves and with the successor of Peter.[37]

---

34. John Paul II, St., *Ordinatio sacerdotalis*, n. 4.

35. Paul VI, *To the committee for the international Year of the Woman*, April 18, 1975.

36. Congregatio Pro Doctrina Fidei, *Responsio ad propositum dubium* (October 28, 1995), in AAS 1995, 1114.

37. The history of *infallibiliter* is complex: "It is in this context that the relatively new notion of the 'hierarchy of truths' appeared. The CDF document of

In addition, the question touches upon the theology of the sacraments, for it looks at the subject of the sacrament of Orders, which is traditionally a man, but does not take into account the presence and role of women in the family and in society as it has developed in the twenty-first century.[38] It is a question of dignity, responsibility and ecclesial participation.

An observation from Fr. Congar

The historical fact of the exclusion of women from priesthood for *impedimentum sexus* is undeniable. However, in 1948, long before the contestations of the 1960s, Fr. Congar taught how "the absence of a fact is not a decisive criterion to conclude prudently that the Church cannot do so and never shall do so."[39]

Also, another theologian adds, "the *consensus fidelium* expressed over many centuries has been called into question in the twentieth century especially in light of the profound sociocultural changes regarding women. It would make no sense to

---

1990 mentions five times the notion of 'truth proposed in a definitive manner' (cfr CDF 1990, § 16 [twice], 17 et 23 [twice], referencing the oath of faithfulness proposed the previous year (Professio 1989), and using a formula of LG 25, *definitivo actu proclamat*. John Paul II's *motu proprio* of 1998, *Ad tuendam fidem*, returns to this question and insists on it once again, modifying the Code of Canon Law at canons 750 and 1371 to introduce this notion. This third category of truths, which come between the truths in which 'I believe' and those to which 'I adhere', gathers the truths that 'I embrace and hold', to use the formula of the oath of faithfulness. This new category of truths astonished quite a few theologians (cfr Sesboue). The matter is not yet entirely brought to light" (B. Pottier, in *ET-Studies* 7 [2016] 117-118).

38. Cfr John XXIII, St., *Pacem in terris* (April 11, 1963), n. 22. For the pope, the role of the woman is one of the connotative phenomena of the modern era. See also T. Beattie, "Simboli infranti. Riflessioni sull' antropologia dei documenti ecclesiastici dal Concilio alla 'Mulieris dignitatem'", in M. Perroni - H. Legrand (eds), *Avendo qualcosa da dire. Teologhe e teologi rileggono il Vaticano II*, Milan, Paoline, 2014, 107-123.

39. P. Congar noted this about the relations between priests and bishops: "Where the Church has done something, we can conclude that she could have and still could do so. But where she has not done something, or where one has no knowledge of what She might have done, it is not always wise to conclude that She cannot and never will do so." Cfr Y. CONGAR, "Faits, problemes et reflexions a propos du pouvoir d'ordre et des rapports entre le presbyterat et l'episcopat", in *La Maison-Dieu* 14 (1948) 128.

maintain that the Church must change only because the times have changed, but it remains true that a doctrine proposed by the Church asks to be understood by the believing intelligence. The debate about women priests could be placed in parallel with other moments in the history of the Church; anyhow, today the *auctoritates*, that is the official positions of the Magisterium, are clear on the question of women's priesthood, but many Catholics struggle to understand the *rationes* of choices which, more than expressions of authority, seem to signify authoritarianism. [...] Today, there is discomfort among those who are unable to understand how the exclusion of women from the ministry of the Church can coexist with the affirmation and valorization of their equal dignity."[40]

The principal issue, resurfacing in the debate, remains: why did the early Church admit some women to the diaconate and even to the apostolate? And why were women then excluded from such functions?

The "grace of the diaconate" for women

Speaking in the general congregations before the 2005 conclave, cardinal Carlo Maria Martini spoke about the possibility of studying the institution of the diaconate for women, given that *Ordinatio sacerdotalis* did not touch upon the question. He recalled that in the early Church there were deaconesses[41] and suggested criteria of discernment that are the same as those of the Second Vatican Council: return to the sources, study the origins, evaluate all in the freedom of being children of God, but especially in rigorous fidelity to the Gospel. This is the same spiritual discernment that is so dear to Pope Francis.

This journal has spoken about the issue many times, and can indicate the contributions of Fr Jean Galot, which date back to the years of the Council and provide an overview on the pre-

---

40. A. Piola, *Donna e sacerdozio*, cit., 8f.

41. He had previously spoken about this at the eucharistic congress in Siena in 1994, "hoping for a serious reflection on the theme of the diaconate," in order to understand the nature and the strength of the presence of women in the Church: cfr *Il Regno-Documenti* 41 (1996) 304.

vious situation.⁴² More recently, Fr. Piersandro Vanzan's article discusses the topic of deaconesses specifically,⁴³ and the author traces their history through post-conciliar publications. The inextricable problem is that of the sacramentality of such roles, in as much as theologians reach opposite conclusions from studying ancient texts. J. Danielou, R. Gryson and C. Vagaggini support a substantial analogy between the ordination of deaconesses and that of deacons.⁴⁴ Meanwhile A. G. Martimort maintains that the ordinations of the eastern deaconesses are to be placed, so to say, half way between the major Orders (diaconate, presbyterate, episcopate) and the wider series of minor ministries (subdiaconate, and those of acolyte and door-keeper, etc.,) which do not involve ordination.⁴⁵

Finally, Fr. Corrado Marucci has faced the intricate problem that sees the presence, functions and sacramentality of women's diaconate in the Church in the first millennium.⁴⁶ He affirms that most studies recognize the ordinations of deaconesses would have had sacramental dignity, and concludes by repeating that "almost all the arguments lead us to consider it very likely that the deaconesses of the ancient and medieval Church received a sacramental ordination analogous to that of deacons."⁴⁷ This is the grace of the diaconate for women.⁴⁸

---

42. Cfr J. Galot, "La missione della donna nella Chiesa", in *Civ. Catt.* 1966 II 16-20; Id., "La donna e il sacerdozio", ivi, 255-263; ID., "L'accesso della donna ai ministeri della Chiesa", in *Civ. Catt.* 1972 II 317-329.

43. Cfr P. Vanzan, "Diaconato permanente femminile. Ombre e luci", in *Civ. Catt.* 1999 I 439-452.

44. Cfr J. Danielou, "Le ministere des femmes dans l'Eglise ancienne", in *La Maison-Dieu* 61 (1960) 70-96; R. Gryson, *Il ministero della donna nella Chiesa antica. Un problema attuale nelle sue radici storiche*, Rome, Citta Nuova, 1974, 124; C. Vagaggini, "Le diaconesse nella tradizione bizantina", in *Il Regno-Documenti* 42 (1987) 672f.

45. Cfr A. G. Martimort, *Les diaconesses...*, cit., 155.

46. Cfr C. Marucci, "Storia e valore del diaconato femminile...", cit., 771-795.

47. Ivi, 792.

48. See the title of A. Borras - B. Pottier, *La grazia del diaconato...*, cit.

Some concluding observations

From what has been said, there is no doubt that the Church had *ordained* deaconesses in the fifth century (Can.15, Council of Chalcedon).[49] Whether that ordination (*cheirotonia*) was considered a sacrament (with the imposition of hands, *cheirothesia*), or only a benediction, or a sacramental is a problem to clarify for the future, keeping in mind the evolution of liturgical terminology.[50] In addition, and above all, there is a need to reply to requests from the second half of the twentieth century to the current time, to recover the women's diaconate.[51] The clarifying word can come from the Magisterium, authoritative interpreter of Tradition. In any case, it is not only a question of returning to the past, as though in the past alone are found indications of the Spirit. Today also, the Lord guides the Church and suggests She courageously assume new outlooks. Besides, the affirmation of Pope Francis cited at the beginning of this article is not limited to what is already known, but is intended to enter into a complex and current field, so that it is the Spirit who guides the Church.

The true problem is not only female diaconate, but the sacramentality of the male diaconate. Some theologians hold that this is implicitly declared in the Council of Trent (DS 1765 and 1776). The Second Vatican Council, in the constitution *Lumen Gentium*, implies that the diaconate is a sacrament: hands are laid on the deacon "not for priesthood, but for service, to be sustained by sacramental grace, [...] in communion with the bishop and his presbytery."[52] Benedict XVI in 2009 with

---

49. Cfr *Conciliorum Oecumenorum Decreta*, Bologna, EDB, 1991, 94.

50. C. Vogel maintains the two terms (*cheirotonia* and *cheirothesia*) are practically equivalent: cfr "Chirotonie et chirothesie. Importance et relativite du geste de l'imposition des mains dans la collation des ordres", in *Irenikon* 45 (1972) 7-21 and 217-238.

51. During the last Synod of Bishops on the family, Mons. P.-A. Durocher, president of the Episcopal Conference of Canada, expressed his hope that the process be opened for the access of women to the diaconate.

52. *Lumen Gentium*, n. 29: "*Diaconi, quibus 'non ad sacerdotium, sed ad ministerium' manus imponuntur. Gratia etenim sacramentali roborati...*" This is mentioned also in the Decree *Ad gentes*, n. 16, and in *Orientalium Ecclesiarum*, n. 17.

the motu proprio *Omnium in mentem* excluded the diaconate from the ministries configured *in persona Christi capitis*. So "the deacons are enabled to serve the people in the diaconate of the liturgy, the word and charity."[53]

The International Theological Commission considers the diaconate a sacramental reality,[54] but it has explicitly excluded women, for according to the tradition of the primitive Church their functions "cannot purely and simply be assimilated to deacons."[55]

Outlook for the future

In the past, and still today, in some Carthusian convents there is a solemn consignment of a diaconal stole by the bishop to allow the superior to preside over the Liturgy of the Hours and proclaim the Gospel in the absence of a priest.[56] The Statutes of the Carthusians define that consignment as "the great sacrament that is fulfilled in solitude, that of Christ and the Church, of which the most eminent example is in the Virgin Mary."[57] This is an important indication of the presence of a female ministry in the Church.

---

53. International Theological Commission, "Il diaconato...", cit., 341 (can. 1009, § 3). Cfr H. Legrand, "*Traditio perpetuo servanda.* La non ordinazione delle donne: tradizione o semplice fatto storico?", in C. Militello (ed.), *Donna e ministero*, cit., 210-213; P. A. Gramaglia, *Le diaconesse*, cit., 673-676.

54. Cfr International Theological Commission, "Il diaconato...", cit., 622.

55. Ivi, 634 f. The text adds that "the unity of the sacrament of orders [...] underlined by ecclesial tradition, especially in the doctrine of the Second Vatican Council and in the post-conciliar teaching of the Magisterium" implies that any ministry of service for women cannot be assimilated to that of sacramental diaconate.

56. Cfr H. Becker - A. Franz, "Die Frau mit der Stola. Zum *Ordo Consecrationis Virginum proprius Monalium Ordinis Cartusiensis* von 1978", in *Theologische Quartalschrift* 192 (2012) 320-328.

57. Ivi, 323.

Protecting Children in the Catholic Church

Hans Zollner, SJ

The issue of sexual abuse of minors committed by clergy is constantly returning to the forefront of media attention. Recently, through various news outlets and publications, this focus has been particularly sustained in Italy, France and Argentina. There is no doubt that the protection of children and youth against sexual violence remains a central problem in the Church, and in society. Catholics who closely identify with the Church and its mission remain deeply disturbed by this.

This concern was expressed once again by the pope on at least two recent occasions: in the conversation with superiors general of male religious orders,[1] and then again, in the preface, which he wrote himself, of a book whose author is a victim of abuse.[2] There, Pope Francis writes: "How can a priest, in the service of Christ and his Church, come to cause such evil? How can one who has consecrated his life to leading the little ones to God, end up instead devouring them in what I have called 'a diabolical sacrifice' which destroys both the victims and the life of the Church? Some victims take their own lives, in the end. These deaths weigh on my heart, on my conscience, and on that of the whole Church. To their families I offer my sentiments of love and sorrow, and I humbly ask forgiveness. It is an absolute monstrosity, a horrendous sin, radically contrary to everything that Christ teaches us."[3]

---

1. Pope Francis, "Take the Gospel without Tranquilizers: A Conversation with the Superiors General", in *Civ. Catt. 0117*, 8-17.
2. Cf. Daniel Pittet, *La perdono, padre,* Milan, Piemme, 2017.
3. The text was reproduced by the popular Italian newspaper *La Repubblica* under the title "Pedophilia, the pope's pain: How can a priest cause so much evil?"

Faced with this horror, complaining is understandable, but the words of the pope call for firm conclusions and commensurate action.

In the coming months and years, more news of this sort will continue to spread – and there will be many such cases, especially if we consider the situation throughout the world. There will be more terrible testimonies of the deliberate or tolerated failures of fundamental pastoral care, both human and Christian. But these will also serve as reminders that demand resolute vigilance. Only when an abscess is cut open and drained can the healing process begin. Without doubt, this process has started very late, after decades, and has not progressed everywhere at the same speed. This is explained somewhat by the fact that the Catholic Church, with its global network of institutions, presents a mix of attitudes and methods adopted to uncover and prevent the sexual abuse of minors.

The universal commitment of the Church to prevent sexual abuse has encountered very different cultural situations. Regarding this challenge, it need only be noted that the Catholic Church has about 1.3 billion followers spread throughout 200 countries, and cannot be construed as a monolithic unit. For example, among these Catholic structures, there are more than 220,000 schools operating in multiple economic, legal, and

---

February 13, 2017. The pope had met Daniel Pittet, author of the book, at the Vatican in 2015, on the occasion of the Year of Consecrated Life. "I could not imagine that this man, so passionate and enthusiastic about Christ, had been the victim of abuse by a priest. And yet," continues the pope, "that's what he told me, and his suffering moved me deeply. I saw once again the tremendous damage caused by sexual abuse, and the long and painful journey that awaits the victims. I am happy that others can read his testimony today and discover how far evil can enter into the heart of a servant of the Church." Daniel chose to meet his tormentor after forty-four years and has reached out: "The wounded child is now," the pope continues, "a man standing – fragile, but standing. I'm very impressed by his words: 'Most people fail to understand that I do not hate. I have forgiven him and I built my life on that forgiveness.' Thank you, Daniel, because this testimony will break down the wall of silence that stifled scandals and suffering, and shed light on a terrible blind spot in the life of the Church. His words open the way to a just healing and grace of reconciliation, and also help pedophiles to become aware of the terrible consequences of their actions."

cultural contexts. The same applies to about 1450 Catholic universities, hundreds of thousands of kindergartens, nursery schools, centers for care of the disabled and for social assistance, hospitals, shelters, and so on. In some countries – for example, Australia, Ireland, Germany, Austria – in reaction to the scandals, the Church has introduced very detailed preventative measures and provides professional training and regulations for employees at every level and in every sector.

But there is also a strong passive resistance which in various local churches moves in the opposite direction with respect to the commitment to discover, intervene in, and prevent sexual abuse. Already from this simple fact, you can see that – contrary to what is perceived and portrayed from the outside – the Catholic Church, at least in this regard, does not have hierarchically structured guidelines or a supervisory structure that would be normal in public administration or in the economic sector.

Pontifical initiatives

However, given what has become clear in the universal Church, the balance has finally shifted slowly but firmly in the right direction. Church leaders at the highest levels, above all Pope Benedict XVI and Pope Francis, have asked us to face seriously the issue of sexual abuse of minors committed by clergy. Even before becoming pope, the then-Cardinal Josef Ratzinger, as prefect of the Congregation for the Doctrine of the Faith, had made a number of significant decisions to tackle cases of abuse. The statute of limitations was extended, in order to protect victims, and abuse against people with mental disabilities likewise came to be considered a crime.

Pope Francis has continued and intensified the line of his predecessor, especially with the establishment of the Pontifical Commission for the Protection of Minors (*Pontificia Commissio pro Tutela Minorum*). He created, at the level of the universal Church, the structural and material conditions needed to accelerate, with consistency and efficiency, the protection of children throughout the Catholic Church. Pope Francis has established the commission as a consultative body on this issue. He has welcomed some proposals of the commission, such as, for example, holding a day of prayer for those who have been victims of abuse, and instituting criminal proceedings against those bishops and religious superiors who silenced or ignored abuse. We have started down the right path, but it is a long and demanding one.

Back in 2011, the Congregation for the Doctrine of the Faith had urged all episcopal conferences to draw up Guidelines for Cases of Sexual Abuse. Large religious orders have also engaged in this task. They must explain, among other things, what is done in individual countries to prevent abuse, how to act with regard to those who have suffered abuse, what legal action to take against the culprits, and what needs to change in priestly formation to prevent abuse.

We continue to ask why there are no uniform guidelines for the whole Church. It should be said in this regard, first of all, that the juridical norms apply, of course, throughout the Catholic Church. This includes the procedures which each bishop must follow in every part of the world in the same way. This starts with a preliminary investigation, and, if it is concluded that the accusations are founded, the case must be submitted to the Congregation for the Doctrine of the Faith in Rome, where it is decided at which level the next steps are to be taken.

Naturally, it would be desirable that these criminal trials take place in the territory of origin. This would facilitate a faster and more transparent process. But this is prevented by the fact that in few local Churches are there canonists in sufficient numbers and properly trained, with a specialization in penal law, and therefore the process cannot be carried out by those with the required expertise. Also worth considering is that the centralization of processes can help prevent the possibility of cover-up by local superiors.

Differing cultural situations

Aside from what for better or worse is the same for all for the universal Church, it should be reiterated that in certain countries we find very different starting situations with regard to cultural views on abuse and its prevention. This includes how sexuality, emotions, and relationships are lived to how they are spoken of or even if they are talked about. The Catholic Church is present in traditionally Confucian countries such as South Korea, and in very conservative countries, as regards sexual relations, such as largely Hindu India. It is in thousands of African cultures, and among the indigenous peoples of the Andean countries.

The meeting of the Christian faith with these many faces of humanity is called inculturation. This influences the celebration of the liturgy and issues with which the Church engages more deeply, such as how to act – or not – towards the thorny issue of sexual abuse of minors committed by clergy. Almost six years since the exhortation by the Congregation for the Doctrine of the Faith, five of the world's 112 episcopal conferences have not yet even established a project to develop their Guidelines for Cases of Sexual Abuse. These are predominately West African francophone conferences.

Also in the realm of civil and criminal law we find different ways of dealing with cases of abuse by state institutions, and this is known to influence the course of action of the Church. An issue frequently debated – and sometimes it happens that in the same country there are different federal states with different norms – is the level of obligation for the individual citizen or for certain professionals to report cases of abuse to the proper authorities. It ranges from the unconditional obligation for those who suspect abuse to report to the police, to intermediate positions – countries where doctors or psychologists can report to the police or report to governmental social services, who may in turn decide whether to report to the police – to states in which there are no specified norms. We must add that in many countries, even when the norms are fixed and defined on paper, they are not considered *really* binding.

In large parts of Africa and Asia, and to some degree Latin America, and parts of Eastern Europe, the sexual abuse of children is still not perceived as an urgent and recurrent problem. This is surprising, because all the statistics clearly show that the sexual abuse of minors is not a rare phenomenon. The figures are, in fact, quite high: 10-15% of boys and 15-20% of girls under the age of 18 are exposed to violence or sexual assault. The most common environment, though also most hidden, is the occurrence of abuse within the family; it raises many urgent questions about how we can help families to live well together, and to foster healthy relationships. In most Southern countries of the world, those who hold positions of responsibility must take the lead in recognizing the problem. In some areas, the idea persists that the sexual abuse of children by clergy is a problem only of the decadent liberal countries of the West.

Let us take a concrete example: the question of prevetion and the protection of children from the perspective of the bishops of the Philippines, and of religious superiors in Rwanda. Listening to them, one learns that these bishops and provincial superiors place the discourse on sexual abuse of children and young people in a different and broader context than is done in richer countries. In poor countries, children and youth suffer brutal treatment of many kinds: those related to war, polluted water, hunger, lack of security, and exploitation of their labor beyond exhaustion. In a world of such violence, suffering sexual assault is a crime not much different than others. Rather, sexual abuse is considered apart of a broader suffering of children and youth. If, therefore, these countries have to establish bodies, both ecclesial and secular, to fight against sexual violence, it must be done in a broader context, aimed at guaranteeing all the rights of childhood. Otherwise you run the risk that the insistence on fighting against sexual abuse be dismissed as Western ideology, which disregards the real-life experience of these countries, often inhumane, and arises from the typically Western neurosis around sexuality.

Increase awareness and commitment to prevention

Despite this, it is possible to say that consciousness of the issue has been raised publicly in the Church, in the center and in the peripheries (to take an expression used by the pope). In Fiji, as in Malawi, in Mexico as in Poland, we now speak openly about abuse in the Church (and at the same time in their respective societies) and its prevention. Many places are now working seriously to deal with cases of abuse, and to realize, or at least to tend toward, prevention. And this prevention is effective, as statistics show. In the United States, where they have taken more severe measures towards prevention than elsewhere, there have been few complaints of abuse committed in recent years. In Germany and Austria, the Catholic Church has issued detailed guidelines for prevention in every diocese, in religious orders, schools, social service centers for the youth, and has put in place corresponding standards for formation and training.

The Church here is setting the standard, and this is recognized also by secular institutions. But it would be dangerous to believe that the task is now completed and that therefore "from now on, everything is just fine." The issue cannot be allowed to fade into the background. First of all, we must continue to deal with cases of abuse in the Church, in society, and in families; it would be an illusion to believe that we can completely eradicate the evil that is done to children only with preventative measures. Second, ongoing commitment to this is a *natural* consequence of the way Jesus behaved with children. This alone should urge those who have responsibility at all levels to do everything possible to protect children.

Without a doubt, over the past five years sensitivity among Church authorities to this issue has increased, as has the willingness to act. But there is not yet everywhere a standing commitment to prioritize the protection of children and young people from sexual abuse, and to manifest this commitment with concrete and effective measures. And this is due to various reasons, one of which may be socio-cultural. The ability to collaborate on the issue of prevention with state institutions or NGOs depends on the position that the Church occupies in each country.

In a predominantly Muslim, Hindu, or Buddhist country, there may or may not be cooperation depending on the degree of tolerance and good will extended by the competent authorities. A case study: In a particular country where Christians make up a small minority and are persecuted by extremists of all kinds, the religious sister who directed an orphanage discovered that a teacher had sexually abused some of the girls. On the basis of her own conscience, bearing in mind the laws of her own country, and considering the obligations toward European sponsors, she wanted and needed to denounce this abuse. However, she did not know how the police would react: the teacher was the mayor's son and both belonged to the dominant religion. The nun thought the police might not react at all, or that any prosecution would have eventually led to the closing down of the orphanage or that the negative publicity would trigger the persecution of Christians under the pretext: "How could the Christians permit this in their institutions?"

The "Centre for Child Protection" at the Gregorian University

Specific prevention programs tend not only to prevent sexual crimes, but also, and above all, make broadly known the conditions, contributing factors, and consequences of sexual abuse, and urge all to act accordingly. In this field, the Church, with its educational, academic, charitable, and pastoral institutions could exercise leadership on a global scale, not only for other religious communities, but for all possible types of bodies and governments, as it does already today in some countries, especially in the global South.

The Centre for Child Protection (CCP) – which carries out its mission at the Pontifical Gregorian University thanks to the generous support of the Archdiocese of Munich and Freising, and the *missio* of the Aachen diocesan *Kindermissionswerk* (the child welfare organization of the Catholic Church in Germany) – is dedicated to the prevention of the abuse of minors.[4] The CCP promotes the work of prevention, primarily in those countries where, so far, little has been done. It also forms people to work for this purpose locally; it offers help for the protection of children and young people to those men and women working in the ecclesial context in parishes, schools, and kindergartens.

How can I tell if a child suffers or has suffered abuse? What can I do to help? What can I do to find out who is guilty? What can I do to create a safe space for children and for young people in a parish or a Catholic school? Combatting sexual abuse is a Herculean task, which requires the collaboration of nearly everyone in the Church and in society. It is a matter of changing how we see and how we act, which, as we know, happens only slowly. This is why the CCP is dedicated to formation: with teaching and training (also available in an e-learning platform, with a certificate in Safeguarding of Minors), research, and the organization of conferences.

The CCP does all this in close collaboration with the Pontifical Commission for the Protection of Minors, especially in the formation of candidates for priesthood and in the formation of leaders in the Church. The CCP intends to offer a lasting impetus to prevention work in the Church, at the universal level, and as a platform for the exchange of ideas and *best practices* in the prevention of abuse, which extends to all countries and continents.

The fight against sexual abuse will endure for a long time, and we have to say goodbye to the illusion that the mere introduction of rules or guidelines is a complete solution. It involves a radical conversion, of adopting the attitude that the commitment to prevention and the decision to bring justice to the victims of abuse will not be set aside when the public attention to the crisis fades.

4. For more information on the CCP, see www.childprotection.unigre.it.

The message of the God of Jesus Christ is the source and strength for this activity, and so reflection continues on the core of the gospel. For God loves above all the small and the vulnerable: "Let the children come to me; do not prevent them, for the kingdom of God belongs to such as these." (*Mk* 10:14, *Mt* 19:14, *Lk* 18:16).

The Border as a Bridge
Migration in Latin America and the Caribbean

Mauricio Garcian Duran, SJ – Gina Paola Sanchez Gonzalez

The issue of migration has been emerging strongly in the last few years as a critical reality in the entire world; it is bringing up major challenges for national governments, for societies and their organizations, and for international institutions.[1] The dynamics of globalization have created a paradoxical situation. While seeing a remarkable opening of national borders for the transit of goods and resources protected by economic agreements and free-trade treaties, we are also witnessing a rigid closure in regards to the crossing of people.

We find ourselves, therefore, in a situation where the world's economic flows are free and protected by international economic agreements, while migratory flows are not protected; rather, they are vulnerable and subject to countless restrictive security policies that threaten human rights.

First, it is important to clarify that "migratory processes have their origin in a variety of causes. Some people emigrate because of the wage gap between the country of destination and the country of origin; others because they are aware of the living conditions in other countries or communities, due to poor governance in their own country, the lack of public services, the low expectations for personal betterment and social and environmental factors, or fear of violence and internal conflicts."[2]

---

1. This text was written and conceived based upon studies and experiences of the Jesuit Network for Migrants from Latin America and the Caribbean (JNM-Lac).

2. R. Cordova Alcaraz – P. Castano Acosta (eds), *Migracion, desarrollo y derechos humanos: la articulacion como base para transformar la realidad social en America Latina y el Caribe*, 2015.

So as to emphasize at the theoretical level the distinction between the causes, one usually refers to "migration" and "forced migration" as two separate phenomena. In practice, however, it is evident that the difference between the former and the latter is increasingly subtle and that the two phenomena are usually interrelated.

To provide an idea about the current status of "forced migration" worldwide, the *Global Trends* report published by the United Nations High Commission for Refugees (UNHCR)[3] informs us that, despite limits and restrictions, in recent years the overall figures related to displaced persons and refugees have been growing rapidly. In 2015, there were 65.3 million people who had been forced to leave their place of origin, either remaining inside their own country or fleeing to another country, which is an increase of over 5 million people from 2014.

These figures certainly have a direct relationship with the crisis prevailing in the Middle East which has generated a large flow of migrants towards Europe, and also indicate that the flows already existing are remaining constant, or even increasing.

Of these, we want to focus on the migratory flow in Latin America and the Caribbean and on the response given by the governments in relation to the globalization process being experienced on the continent.

The Mexico-USA border and the "Northern Triangle"

In regard to Latin America, it is known that a historic and very substantial flow is that of the Mexican population to the United States. In 2012, the number of Mexicans in the USA amounted to more than 33 million people.[4] This figure results

---

3. UNCHR, *Tendencias Globales. Desplazamiento forzado en 2015: forzados a huir*, 2016. Cf www.acnur.org

4. See Observatorio Iberoamericano sobre Movilidad Humana Migraciones y Desarrollo (Obimid), *Las migraciones en las fronteras en Iberoamerica*, by A. Ares Mateos – J. Eguren Rodriguez, Madrid, Comillas, 2016.

from a variety of reasons, including the economic situation, drug trafficking, the constant threat of violence and low wages. From a retrospective and historical point of view, the flow of migrants has also been influenced by a definition of the borders between the two countries that does not necessarily correspond to cultural, social and economic dynamics of the population that lived and lives near the border.

It is important to emphasize that if the Mexican trend continues consistently, according to the latest research of the Jesuit Network for Migrants from Latin America and the Caribbean published in a report from Obimid,[5] the most critical situation at this time has to do with the increasing migration from what is referred to as the "Northern Triangle."[6] In looking at the details, it is alarming to see that the great majority of these migrants are represented by children and adolescents. According to the cited study, between January and November 2014, Mexico had 21,547 migrant children and adolescents, 178% more than the same period in 2013; 43% of these were Honduran, 34% Guatemalan and 22% Salvadoran.[7]

It is well known that the Central American *corridor* is of great economic importance for North America and that there is a large flow of goods passing through this region that fuels the economy of the continent. But, even though the route had been established for the legal transit of goods, it has already become just as important for drug trafficking, human trafficking and for illegal activities in general. Due to the ambiguity of the corridor, some outstanding issues such as the fight against drug trafficking and terrorism by the United States have led to a series of security policies known as the so-called "policies of the 'extended border' in the Northern Triangle." These interventions do not respond to the needs of the migrants and actually threaten their fundamental rights,

---

5. Ibid.
6. The name conventionally used to identify the region encompassing Guatemala, Honduras and El Salvador.
7. See Obimid, *Las migraciones en las fronteras en Iberoamerica*, cit.

creating more stringent control mechanisms and forcing them to find other routes which are often unfamiliar, and therefore more dangerous.

The Caribbean: the flow of Haitians

Without forgetting the others, the predominant flow in this geographical area goes from Haiti to the Dominican Republic. It is a historical movement resulting from natural disasters and from the political and economic conditions of Haiti. In recent years, this flow has grown considerably in numbers, which has made it a priority for the various non-governmental organizations operating in the region. In fact, it is estimated that in 2012, Haitian migrants in the Dominican Republic represented 87% of all the migrants present in the country,[8] the vast majority of whom were illegal.

But, apart from size, the Haitian migratory flow gained particular attention as a result of policies of the government of the Dominican Republic in the last four years. In 2013, the Dominican government, with the 168/13 ruling – a decision that retroactively changed the regulations in place since 1929[9] – withdrew the nationality of about 250,000 Dominican residents of foreign origin, particularly Haitians. The provision considerably increased the number of foreign migrants in the territory and aggravated the lack of legal protection since it stripped away all legal rights to citizenship. In the year following this drastic intervention, the ruling became law. The legislation was supposed to cushion the impact of the mechanism described above, but implementation did not have this desired result.

Subsequently, in 2015, the Dominican government launched a "National Plan for the Legalization of Foreigners" (NPLF), so that immigrants established in the country could legalize

---

8. According to the first national survey on immigrants in the Dominican Republic, conducted by the United Nations in 2012.

9. See R. Cordova Alcaraz – P. Castano Acosta (eds), *Migracion, desarrolloy derechos humanos...*, cit.

their resident status. However, the implementation of this plan encountered many obstacles. Many immigrants were unable to legalize in time, resulting in only about 288,000 successfully registering. This is a large figure in absolute terms, but not when viewed in consideration of the substantial Haitian population in the Dominican Republic. Added to this situation were the repeated violations of the ban on deportations during the implementation of the NPLF, deportations that took place without any control.

Between Colombia and Venezuela

In previous years, the migratory flows in this area were determined by armed Colombian conflict which resulted in internal displacement and migration to neighboring countries in search of international protection. However, the flows are changing now, in particular as a result of border closings by the Venezuelan government, which triggered a serious humanitarian crisis.

As if this were not enough, besides the obvious violations of the rights of the Haitian population, very blatant xenophobic practices began to spread, and people of Haitian origin had more reasons to leave the Dominican Republic and look elsewhere for greater economic opportunities. This included Brazil and Chile, where, however, the migrants faced not only a lack of legal recognition, but also a different language and a lack of cultural and social recognition. In the past year, the economic crisis and Brazilian politics led to a preference for migration towards Chile, although it is possible to find Haitian migrants in transit in Central America and in Colombia.

Since July 2015, the Venezuelan security forces have carried out more than 135 operations, including some raids in well-populated communities, as a part of the "Operation for the Liberation and Protection of the People" (OLP), an intervention which resulted in deportations reaching their peak in August 2015. It must be noted that this type of action was justified in two ways: the fight against criminal gangs, which had increased the rate of violence in Venezuela, and the liberation of the country from armed groups and the political Right.[10]

According to the most recent report on the humanitarian situation on the border between Colombia and Venezuela, prepared by the "United Nations Office for the Coordination of Humanitarian Affairs" (OCHA), of the 24,292 repatriated Colombians, 1,950 are to be considered as deported. Specifically, the regional distribution is as follows: Norte de Santander (18,770 repatriated / 1,109 deported), Vichada (193 repatriated / 1 deported), La Guajira (1,938 repatriated / 739 deported), Arauca (1,441 repatriated / 101 deported). In other words, many people emigrated due to the armed conflict in Colombia. In repatriating them their refugee status was not respected, violating their rights and the legislation that protects them.

On the Venezuelan front, it is surprising that, given the political, economic and social situation of the country, a flow of Venezuelans to Colombia has begun in spite of the closing of the border by the government in Caracas. Although there is no explicit armed conflict in Venezuela, people have decided to migrate due to the economic crisis, the scarcity of food, the level of violence, political radicalization and the feeling of not having any prospects in their own country.

South America: intraregional flows and "circular migration"

In regard to southern Latin America, the principal countries of destination for the various migratory flows are Brazil, Chile and Argentina. This part of the continent has been historically characterized by the phenomenon of having intraregional flows, caused by the presence of an indigenous population living in a region – the plateau – which transcends national borders and the economic dynamics

---

10. SJR-LAC – SJR-Colombia, *Balance de la situacion en frontera posterior a la emergencia humanitarian*, 2016.

related to labor needs. This can be observed at border crossings: an example is the passage from Chacalluta-Santa Rosa, on the border between Chile and Peru, where Peruvians go to Arica to work and the Chileans travel to Tacna to consume goods and to take advantage of services and medical care because of the favorable exchange rate. Similarly, between Tacna and Arica, and even between Arica and Oruro or La Paz, it is normal to have a "circular migration," in which people go from one side of the border to the other on a daily basis for work or for other economic reasons.

However, there are exceptions to this natural tendency towards human mobility in the region. The area of the Amazon and border crossings such as Desaguadero – between Peru, Chile and Bolivia – that are void of controls, have become very popular corridors for migrants rejected elsewhere and for victims of human trafficking, primarily Afro-Colombians and Dominicans, men and women. These flows represent a major challenge for the various countries involved.

Similarly, following the 2010 earthquake in Haiti, the number of Haitian citizens who left the country due to the humanitarian and political crisis has grown exponentially. It has been calculated that there are 80,000 Haitians in Brazil and, even though there are no studies or official data, the Jesuit Service for Migrants of Chile is constantly welcoming more Haitians coming from Brazil who report that in that country, although they encounter less xenophobia than in Chile, there are still fewer job opportunities.

From borders as limits to borders as bridges

As might be guessed from this quick rundown of some of the primary migratory flows in Latin America, the dynamic of migration is in itself complex and its causes and consequences are diverse. It is clear, however, that there is movement in a paradoxical way towards a combination of free trade policies and restrictive immigration policies. This means that we are faced with a halfway globalization which, combined with the dynamics of an illegal economy (drug trafficking, human trafficking, arms smuggling, etc.), ends up aggravating the very critical social situation at the root of the growing migratory flows.

Far from seeing a solution to these processes, let us begin then to identify the enormous challenges that invite us to stop looking at borders as limits that create differences, divide and at times pit populations against each other, and begin to think of these same borders as bridges of interaction which permit the formation of "cross-border subjects," open to intercultural dynamics, promoters of their territory and contributors to a just, inclusive and fraternal society.

Venezuela: The Misery of King Midas

Arturo Peraza, SJ

How does an oil-rich nation like Venezuela, enjoying one of the most advantageous geographical locations in continental America and having achieved a high level of development in the second half of the twentieth century, turn into a society on its knees, begging for humanitarian aid, medicine, and food? How is it possible for one of the first representative democracies in Latin America to become so bitterly divided?

The fate of Venezuela brings to mind the myth of King Midas: a man who could turn anything into gold just by touching it, but who also ended up miserable, unable even to feed himself. It is true that there is an abundance of black gold in Venezuela, but just like Midas, the blind faith that led Venezuelans to believe that petroleum was the one and only resource for sustenance also led them to a serious condition of collective poverty.

An attempt to describe the situation

The most complicated question in Venezuela is how anyone can come to an agreement on anything, including the very causes of the country's ills. Political conflict has become so acrimonious that any attempt to identify the causes is automatically labeled as tendentious by those being blamed. Nevertheless, we must take an honest look at the daily life of Venezuelans.

Celebrating Sunday Eucharist in one of the most heavily populated and poorest sections of Caracas opens a window onto several aspects of the problem. In the *San Blas* section of the *Petare* quarter (one of the largest suburban areas in all

Latin America), people talk about the lines they must wait in for the necessities of life: rice, flour, sugar, coffee, pasta, red meat and poultry, margarine, and other produce fundamental to the Venezuelan diet. They have to endure similar lines to buy bread and personal hygiene products (toothpaste, shampoo, soap, etc.). It is even worse when it comes to medicine, for it is quite normal for a pharmacist to say that there simply is not any more available.

In such situations of dire shortage, parallel markets inevitably spring up, charging exorbitant prices for their goods. In Venezuela, these markets are called *bachaquero* because transporting goods across the border (contraband) is a very lucrative business: indeed, the person who traffics the goods is called a *bachaquero*. The problem lies in the fact that, since the Venezuelan economy is closed to foreign exports, every transaction with a neighboring country is considered contraband, and the Venezuelan border is large and difficult to control.

For this reason, citizens must make a choice: they either go to the official markets and stand in day-long lines in order to buy goods at relatively affordable prices, or they buy them through illegal *bachaquero* at virtually unaffordable prices. The result is the same, especially for the poor: hunger.

Organizations such as *Cendas* report that in the month of October 2016, a monthly portion of basic nutritional goods for a family of five cost 429,626 Bolivars (VEF, the official exchange rate is VEF9.98 to USD1).[1] The minimum monthly wage is VEF 65,056. So a family of five must earn at least 6.6 times the minimum monthly wages to acquire basic nutrition. It is not easy to find trustworthy data on the situation of poverty in Venezuela. A study conducted by one of the most prestigious universities

---

1. Cf. "*Cendas: Canasta Basica se ubico en Bs. 429,626 en octubre*," in www.globovision.com, 21 November 2016.

in the country placed the poverty level at 73%.[2] The National Institute of Statistics, a government agency, sets it at 33%.[3]

Long lines have an impact on every aspect of daily life in Venezuela. Teachers (who are paid terribly) must skip school when it is their turn to stand in line. Many workers have to do the same thing. The reasoning is the same: "if I don't go to the store today, I will have nothing to feed my children." In a country that used to enjoy abundance in almost everything, this creates an atmosphere of anxiety, anger, and frustration; a collective spirit that, from a social viewpoint, is entirely unhelpful and extremely dangerous.

Such feelings, together with other factors, have caused crime rates to run rampant. The incidence of violent crime in Venezuela is the highest in Latin America.[4] This generates a constant state of insecurity in every city of the nation, especially in the capital, Caracas. The city's streets are already empty from 7 p.m. or 8 p.m. onwards. Those who go out in the early morning place themselves at great risk, but they often have no other choice, because to commute from residential areas to the commercial centers takes from one-and-a-half to two hours. It is risky to carry a smartphone in Caracas regardless of whether you are in your own car or on public transportation: in either case, you expose yourself to thieves who are always armed. Stories of delinquent youths getting onto public transportation and robbing passengers are endless; they are recounted like heroic battles where victory is to escape unharmed.

A word about the problem of internal division is also in order. Venezuela has immersed itself in a political process that has attempted, not without success, to divide the population between those in support of *comandante* Hugo Chavez Frias' program and those opposed to it. I should add that any poll

---

2. Cf. *"Encovi: Mas de 3 millones de venezolanos comen dos veces al dia o menos,"* in www.efectococuyo.com, 31 March 2016.

3. Cf. *"Crece pobreza en Venezuela, segun informe del INE,"* in www.elnacional.com, 26 August 2016.

4. Cf. *"Informe del observatorio venezolano de violencia 2015,"* in www.eluniversal.com.

today will reveal that such a division does not exist; people are simply concerned with their own survival. But in the arena of political power and scheming, an increasingly bitter division is causing great harm to the solidarity of the citizens.

In the election of December 2015, the opposition made considerable gains, giving it total control of Parliament. The high court of justice subsequently declared a suspension of three parliamentarians who had been elected to represent the state of Amazzonia, but the National Assembly decided they should assume their duties despite the court's decision. The regime then tried to isolate Parliament and deprive it of its functions. In turn, the opposition, maneuvering to protect the gains it had made, took decisions against the constitutional framework. Now a process of negotiation has begun, and the Holy See has entered the picture as a companion collaborator. How did things get to this point?

The revenue from Venezuelan oil

The story of Venezuela can be divided into two main chapters: before oil, and after oil. Oil was stamped onto this nation's history in the 1920s and has determined its economic model ever since: an economic model which, in turn, has generated its political systems. We might even call it "oil revenue" not only in economic terms, but also in profoundly cultural terms.

"Oil revenue" has also molded the political, social, economic, and cultural relationship between Venezuelan society and the State. This income is based on the State's foray into oil extraction as its owner but without balancing this foray with labor and productivity.

Basically, the entire life of Venezuelan society depends on the distribution of this oil revenue by the State. With the funds, available to it, Venezuela acquires all the goods and services needed for its sustenance: a phenomenon difficult to explain when one considers that vast tracts of land are available for crops and livestock.

Oil revenue has progressively imposed itself as the country's one economic resource and has gradually led the State to its role as the sole arbitrator in society. The relationship that successive Venezuelan governments have established with the people is thus one of *clientelism*: in other words, the government purchases the favor of the people and its own democratic legitimacy by how it distributes that revenue. And that distribution has never been egalitarian: some end up privileged depending on which interest groups the government wishes to favor. That notwithstanding, political conflicts have generally been resolved by a redistribution of revenue. Whoever reaches a higher level of political influence is guaranteed a larger share of the revenue, which functions as a sort of *bozal de arepa*, a tranquillizing pill.[5]

For this reason, politics reign supreme in Venezuela: it is not a matter of one power among others, but, in practice, of one single power: whoever governs the country governs the State, and whoever governs the State holds control of the revenue upon which the entire society depends. When the revenue is high, so is the popularity of the government; when it is low, the popularity of the government is also low.

A good example of this can be found in president Carlos Andres Perez (1974-79 and 1989-93). During his first term, oil revenue sprang from $4 a barrel to $32 a barrel. From the polls conducted at the time, never has there been a more popular president than Perez. His establishment of a "Great Venezuela" made him so famous that when he ran for the presidency again in 1989, he won by a huge margin, even though the social conditions of that time were quite different: the price of oil had considerably fallen and a large debt loomed over the Venezuelan treasury. Perez, thinking he could win the people over simply by his own prestige, proposed a program of austerity (and therefore a reduction in oil wealth distribution) that resulted in a popular uprising known as *Caracazo*[6] and turned Perez into one of the most hated politicians in the nation's history.

---

5. The Venezuelan phrase *Bozal de arepa* refers to the corn that is typical of the country's diet: *arepa*.

6. Literally, "Scandal of Caracas." The suffix "-azo" increases the negative connotation.

This, in turn, led to the so-called "Bolivarian Revolution" of the twenty-first century. The one who launched it considers it a Marxist, socialist revolution, and considers Bolivar's thought socialist (even if not Marxist, given that Bolivar lived before Marx). All in all, it is considered a revolution aimed at repairing unjust structures in Venezuelan society by modifying the socio-economic model of production.

In reality, the revolution brought no change of economic or cultural model. Using Marxist categories, we could conclude that, if there was no modification of the model of production (or of revenue in the economic sense), there was in fact no revolution. We could say that it was nothing more than a cosmetic intervention, a change in the name of the political superstructure that is the State without any real change.

In an article written in 2007, the current Superior General of the Jesuits, Arturo Sosa, asserts that "the economic model being constructed in Venezuela closely resembles a capitalism of the State, with the caveat that the State has a lot of money from oil production: in other words, from the exploitation of a non-renewable natural resource. This important cash flow entering the national budget without any connection to the productive activity of society and with no tie to economic productivity is utilized by the State for massive public expenditures and very little is destined for public investment. The primary role of the Venezuelan state is more one of distributing revenue than of redistributing wealth generated by the wider society. The State promotes endogenous revenue dependent on foreign markets both for its income and its investments." [7]

Both high oil revenue and an unquestionable talent for charismatic leadership fueled Hugo Chavez's popularity. At the same time, the political chaos that erupted in 2013 was due precisely to a fall in oil prices and the simultaneous physical disappearance of Chavez and entrance of the current president, Nicolas Maduro Moros.

---

7. Cf. A. Sosa, "*El proceso político venezolano 1998-2007*," in *Sic* 70 (2007), 487-506.

Just as with president Perez, the people's enchantment or disenchantment with their leader appears connected to the distribution of revenue. It is worth pointing out that the cycle of oil revenue has certain constants: in fact, oil prices rise in cycles of approximately five to seven years while periods of recession last from ten to fifteen years. It is similar to the story of Joseph in the Old Testament: there are times when the livestock are fat and times when they are thin. In any case, Venezuela, even though aware of these fluctuations, had no Joseph ensuring grain be stored.

Thus the relationship between Venezuelan society and oil is dysfunctional, and this has left the country in a productivity vacuum (though not an absence of work). It matters little how much or little the private sector produces in other ways, because such production has little bearing on the national economy, which basically depends on oil revenue. The State does not promote private industry, but – in ways more or less pronounced throughout history – it restricts it to the internal market.

In the last phase of the so-called "Bolivarian revolution," private industry suffered a blow and was sidelined because it was considered an undesirable economic outgrowth. Consequently, the imposed economic model has simply reinforced a capitalism of the State. The government has intervened to expropriate various private enterprises in different sectors of the economy (cement, sugar, livestock, electricity, food-grade oil, ready-made flour, rice, etc.): in the following years, all these sectors have invariably suffered losses and a decrease in productivity.

The final result has been a sort of economic catastrophe with deplorable results, starting with the closure of the automobile industry (91% of its production) in 2016.[8] Figures offered by various trade organizations in 2015 show that in recent years there has been a closure of 7,000 industries and small

---

8. Cf. *"Conindustria: En Venezuela estamos ante el cierre total de la industria automotriz,"* in all footnote on previous page www.el-nacional.com (8 November 2016).

businesses.[9] The president of *Conindustria,* an industrial association, has affirmed two thirds of industrial enterprises in Venezuela failed to survive.[10] According to statistics provided by the central bank of Venezuela, inflation between June 2015 and June 2016 was 487.6%, the highest in the country's economic history.[11]

The magazine *Sic* and the Gumilla Center, both organs of the Venezuelan church and directed by the Jesuits, have repeatedly underscored the need to overcome the model of cliental revenue that dominates the country's socio-economic and political systems in favor of a model that builds the nation's wealth on the basis of labor and productivity. But the temptation to redistribute oil wealth as a way of political compromise is great and makes transition very difficult.

Deinstitutionalizing the State

The cliental relationship ends up generating processes that break down the State's power since access to national works and services becomes detached from a normative system and instead caters to individual interests. This phenomenon has a long history in Venezuela, but during the so-called "revolutionary process" it has reached paroxysmal levels.

Unfortunately, the history of Venezuela is riddled with coups d'etat and constitutional reforms (there have been twenty-three constitutions in the republic's history) designed to favor the interests of whichever group assumes power. There have been many times when a constitutional norm has been changed instead of simply amending an article of the civil, penal, or commercial legal codes. It is difficult to maintain "institutionality" if fundamental norms are tampered with by the capriciousness of whoever wields power.

9.Cf. *"Aseguran que siete mil industrias han cerrado en Venezuela,"* in www.eluniversal.com (25 June 2015).
10.Cf. *"En el 2017 se agravara crisis economica y continuara la mortandad de industrias,"* in www.conindustria.org (13 December 2016).
11.Cf. *"El primer semestre cerro con inflacion de 176,2%,"* in www.el-nacional.com (11 July 2016).

By the term institutionality we refer to relations between citizens and the power structure – in this case the State – mediated by a respect for norms that regulate those relations and establish a relationship of equality among the citizens that is indeed the foundation of any republican system. Norms grant a necessary, basic – albeit insufficient – minimum formal equality that, within the framework of the Church's social teaching, must be accompanied by an equality of opportunity and distributive justice. Institutions help to limit the risk that power might be exercised in a merely discretional way and they give rise to elements that favor judicial security and monitor abuses. In this sense, institutionality is a necessary good.

None of this can be taken for granted in Venezuela. The revolution maintains that the existing institutionality favored oligarchical groups and, like every revolution, it strives to create a new institutional framework it calls socialist. But in fact, the constitution approved at the beginning of this process in 1999 is ill-suited and restrictive. This is because in reality the Chavist project is a political model that would better be defined as populist and a cult of personality: something that has become endemic to Latin America as exemplified in the lives of Juan and Evita Peron and Vargas.

Today there is talk of a "new populism" as revealed in the governments of Fujimori and Chavez. The key to interpreting this phenomenon is the fact that, rather than choosing an institutional framework (furnished with political parties and structures), the chosen leader represents in some way the popular masses. This leader takes on the role of a semi-sovereign in the sense that sovereignty rests with the people who, through elections, delegates it to the elected president. The elected figure, even though he seems to subordinate himself to the structures of the liberal State, is radically detached from them as he proposes a need for social transformation that he himself represents, assumes, promotes, and puts into action. In this way, the other powers of the State become mere mechanisms of the one who holds power.

Here we might introduce an example based on a very delicate topic. According to the Constitution of 1999, the armed forces are an essentially professional institution without political militancy that, in carrying out their functions, are at the service solely of the nation and not any particular person or political party.[12] It could be said that all of this is normal, but at all official ceremonies the soldiers must greet and take their leave with the phrase "*Chavez vive, la Patria sigue*" (Chavez lives, the Homeland must march onward.)[13] At the same time, in many other cases, in official ceremonies the soldiers have expressed their adherence to a political group that happened to be in power at the time. All of this has led to a gradual loss of a sense of the armed forces as an institution according to the 1999 Constitution.

The same thing has happened in the case of other public entities of power. The Supreme Tribunal of Justice has not issued a sentence against the executive power in over twelve years. Until 2015, Parliament was dominated by the governing party, and throughout its mandate, it gave special powers to presidents Chavez and Maduro. Once the opposition finally took control of Parliament after its victory in the 2015 election, the Supreme Tribunal of Justice issued a series of rulings that nullified every single act of Parliament without exception as long as the three

---

12. *The Constitution of the Bolivarian Republic of Venezuela*, art. 328: "The National Armed Forces constitute an essentially professional institution, with no political orientation, organized by the State to guarantee the independence and sovereignty of the Nation and ensure the integrity of its geographical space, through military defense, cooperation for the purpose of maintaining internal order and active participation in national development, in accordance with this Constitution and the law. In performing their functions, they are at the exclusive service of the Nation, and in no case at the service of any person or political partisanship. The pillars on which they are founded are discipline, obedience and subordination. The National Armed Forces consist of the Army, the Navy, the Air Force and the National Guard, which function in an integrated manner within the scope of their competence to fulfill their mission, with their own overall Social Security system, as established under the pertinent organic law." Cf. www.mp.gob.ve/LEYES/constitucion/constitucion1.html.

13. See for example this 2012 note (written when president Chavez was still alive): "*Chavez reitera energicamente que la Fanb es 'bolivariana, revolucionaria, socialista y chavista,*'" in www.noticias24.com.

members of Parliament from Amazzonia, who had been suspended by the court, were permitted to function.

This absence of institutionality has grown worse during the mandate of the current president, Maduro. The promulgation of an emergency economic decree – of dubious legitimacy in that it did not receive the necessary approval of Parliament – was an arbitrary intrusion into several facets of the country's economy. But use was made of such emergency decrees to pass legislation on almost any question regarding the life of the nation and with the implicit suppression of all powers of Parliament.

Moreover, these last years in Venezuela have witnessed arbitrary imprisonments of a political nature[14] and, in some cases, a complete disregard for the Constitution and the principle of due process. The trial of the dissident Leopoldo Lopez, for example, is generally considered null.[15] Some of those detained had been elected representatives in the National Assembly and thereby deserved parliamentary immunity, a right completely ignored by the government.

When the rule of law is not maintained in a State, the situation becomes anarchical. The law loses its force, impunity flourishes, and the sense of social responsibility is lost. This situation has had an impact on the soaring crime rate. Many Venezuelans live in a constant state of fear and insecurity. The death rate from violent crime is one of the world's highest: in 2015, 90 out of every 100,000 citizens died a violent death.[16] In response to this grave situation, the State launched an urban safety program called *Operacion de Liberacion del Pueblo* (OLP) that, in the end – as several important human rights advocates have noted – has

---

14. See the opinion of the United Nations Council of Human Rights working-group on arbitrary imprisonments, *"Detencion arbitraria / Venezuela: Expertos de la ONU exigen liberacion inmediata de Leopoldo Lopez,"* in www.ohchr.org (18 September 2015).

15. Cf. the note of the inter-American Commission on Human Rights (CIDH) in number 75 of its 2015 Annual Report, in www.oas.org.

16. Cf. *"2015 Tasa de homicidios llego a 90 por cada 100 mil habitants,"* in www.observatoriodeviolencia.org.ve (18 February 2016).

been transformed into a system of extra-judicial executions.[17] In short, faced with a situation of anarchy, the State's response has been, in turn, equally anarchical. The situation is even grimmer when we look at statistics regarding the Venezuelan penal system.[18]

The process of deinstitutionalization, the disintegration of the rule of law, and grave violations of human rights have been denounced by various international organizations. We only have to look at the recommendations made by the United Nations' Council for Human Rights,[19] the declarations of its High Commission for Human Rights,[20] or the above-cited Inter-American Commission on Human Rights, which for more than ten years has been publishing reports on the situation in Venezuela.

The existence of a democratic institutionality within the framework of a rule of law – implying a distinction between public powers and the definition of their functions, as well as a respect for the human rights of all citizens regardless of political views and social class – is an indispensable prerequisite for opening a process of reconciliation based on the principle of justice that permits Venezuelans to overcome the current crisis.

Paths to reconciliation and justice

It will not be possible to overcome the present situation if no agreement is reached between the government and various political, social, and economic actors. It is a grave situation further complicated by the fact that problems have always been dealt with through confrontation. In the meantime, poverty and social exclusion are on the rise. The Venezuelan Church has

---

17. Cf. "*Provea: OLP criminaliza la pobreza y viola los DDHH en Venezuela,*" in www.actualidadygente.com.
18. See the 2014 Report "*Observatorio Venezolano de Prisiones,*" in oveprisiones.org.
19. Cf. Universal Periodic Review, "Venezuela 2016 Recommendations," in www.upr-info.org/database.
20. Cf. "*Comisionado de DDHH critico a Venezuela por negar acceso a sus funcionarios,*" in www.eluniversal.com (13 September 2016).

repeatedly and explicitly made this clear through the teaching of its Episcopal Conference. For example, a pastoral exhortation published in January of 2016 states: "Faced with the current reality of our country, the light of the Gospel and the words of Pope Francis invite us to look closely at our concrete situation. We exhort all political authorities to fulfill their duties, to respect the autonomy due to each of the powers, to search for forms of genuine dialogue that address the actual problems of the people rather than secondary or peripheral issues that only waste time and energy, or lead to rigid positions and sterile confrontation."[21]

On various occasions, Pope Francis has invited the people and leaders of Venezuela to build up a culture that overcomes strife through dialogue and reconciliation. We only have to look at his *Urbi et Orbi* address on Easter Sunday in 2016: "With the weapons of love, God has defeated selfishness and death. His son Jesus is the door of mercy open wide to all. May his Easter message be felt ever more powerfully by the beloved people of Venezuela in the difficult conditions which they are experiencing, and by those responsible for the country's future, that everyone may work for the common good, seeking spaces of dialogue and cooperation with all. May efforts be made everywhere to promote the culture of encounter, justice and reciprocal respect, which alone can guarantee the spiritual and material welfare of all people!"

In fact, these words did not stay merely at the abstract level of an exhortation. Since October 2016, the Holy See, through a delegate appointed by the Pope himself – Archbishop Claudio Maria Celli – has tried to collaborate as a companion in the dialogue underway in Venezuela to find negotiated solutions to the current political and humanitarian crisis.

These are complex negotiations that will probably not lead to any simple solution. As in every process there will be cliffs, dark valleys, dangerous curves and wrong turns. But the

---

21."*Venezuela realizo el encuentro de delegados de la pastoral de medios de comunicacion*," in www.cev.org.ve (10 March 2016).

alternative – resolving problems through violence – is unacceptable to the Church.

Besides concrete political negotiations, it is necessary to seek basic agreements that would give Venezuela a new start. It is neither desirable nor even possible to return to the past. On the other hand, the current political system has proven to be impracticable and democratically unsustainable. In terms of sheer politics, no alternative appears on the horizon.

Negotiating a way out for Venezuela will involve much more than effecting agreements between political power brokers to resolve disagreements over how to keep power in check. Negotiating means establishing a new social pact on which a new model of development can be built – a model that goes beyond "extractionism" or a kind of development based solely on the extraction of underground resources. Another system is needed that promotes the growth of the citizens, their work, and their investment. This will require establishing an objective and transparent institutional framework for utilizing public revenue, and a recognition of the right of citizens to organize themselves freely without restraint from political groups that abuse their efforts. It will entail a strengthening of the social fabric and social services.

It is for this reason that the Holy See's gamble – a gamble of dialogue – embodies a vision that transcends the current circumstances and foresees a way out for Venezuela. There is still time to embark on this journey. The situation could be worse. It is not like the war in Colombia or the ten-year horror that shook Central America. There are still flickers of life that might set the light of liberty aflame.

Louis Lebret
The Legacy of the Mentor of *Populorum Progressio*

Fernando de la Iglesia Viguiristi, SJ

July 20, 2016 was the fiftieth anniversary of the death of Fr. Louis Lebret. This Dominican from Brittany is not very well-known. However, we have no doubt that the grand mentor of *Populorum Progressio* deserves attention and study. Therefore, in this article we will discuss his life, thought and spirituality, providing a contribution towards recognizing the value of his legacy.

Life

Louis Lebret was born on June 26, 1897 to a family linked to the sea, in the town of Minihic sur Rance, close to Saint-Malo, in the French region of Brittany. His father was the head shipwright at a naval shipyard. After having studied mathematics in high school, Louis enrolled in the Naval Academy. In 1917, with the war in full force, he was already an assistant officer to the captain on a torpedo-boat. In 1920 he became an instructor of navy officers at the Brest School. He was soon sent to Beirut, where he was put in charge of port traffic. At 23 years of age he was named Knight of the Legion of Honor and had reached the rank of lieutenant. As we see, he took on important responsibilities from a young age, and had the opportunity to demonstrate his enterprising character.

Louis Lebret's intention to enter the clergy gradually developed during those years in the Navy. After abandoning his brilliant career as a naval officer, he became a Dominican. He completed his novitiate in Angers and studied philosophy and theology in Rijckholt, Holland. For health reasons, during the last year of his studies, he was sent to the convent of Saint-Malo for a period of convalescence.

He thus returned to his native land, by the seashore, and there he encountered a reality that was very close to him, but that he had not been aware of before: that of the local fishermen, who lived in poverty, almost destitution, and lacked a minimum level of dignity. In order to offer them spiritual assistance, he founded the Christian Maritime Youth, but soon recognized the limits of this initiative, and after a period of time, he succeeded in founding the French Federation of Professional Seamen Unions with the collaboration of Ernest Lamort. From 1932 to 1939 he published a trade union newspaper *La Voix du Marin*. For more than ten years he dedicated all his efforts and energies to the question of the fishermen and related sectors. His activities developed on two levels: *1)* putting pressure on the institutions to improve laws; *2)* carrying out direct work with the fishermen involved.

This period of the Saint-Malo movement was very important in the life of Fr. Lebret. We can see every aspect of his method of operating. First of all, it should be noted that, at the origin and heart of every initiative he undertook throughout his life, the fundamental motivation was always evangelical mercy. This explains what Fr. Lebret did and brings unity to all his dynamic activities. Sociology, human economy and economic development had no meaning for him, except in relation to those who lived in degrading conditions, from which they must be removed, leading to their progress.

For Fr. Lebret mercy was not a synonym for paternalism or alms-giving. And it was also not a correction to be made to an unjust world. It was much more than taking an interest in unfortunate people; it was experiencing the same fate with them. Whoever is touched by this sentiment, is branded and cannot but actively fight to help people who suffer. The more he does, the more he sees how much work is necessary in the great task of eliminating all misery.

Taking care of others requires a strong will and decisive love with which the activist takes responsibility for a concrete group of humans before God and before his own conscience. He joins them, enters their lives, and hopes to be accepted as one of them. It is a phenomenon of merging, of letting oneself be absorbed.

In his native land Fr. Lebret concluded the first application of the method he would follow in all of his subsequent activities: his celebrated investigations. He tirelessly repeated that it was necessary to start with the facts. In his view, nothing could substitute for direct and systematic observation. Starting there, it became possible to think of what should be done, and to outline the concrete actions to be taken.

As a child of St. Dominic and St. Thomas, he was a man of deep education and was very thoughtful. He aimed to ensure that everything he did was based on solid principles. His famous research sessions began at Saint-Malo. That was when he realized that it was necessary to get at the roots of evil, after having studied its causes.

Fr. Lebret knew how to identify key people and educate them. For him, collaborating with the laity was as natural as it was necessary. He surrounded himself with great figures, like Ernest Lamort. It was unquestionable in his view that temporal problems required solutions of the same temporal order. Since those solutions needed to be well-grounded, he concentrated all of his knowledge and energies on this point, carrying out sociological investigations, statistical analyses and economic studies that allowed him to formulate resolute strategy and tactics. This is what we find in the *Voix du Marin,* the paper *that* he inspired.

In a period of full economic crisis, there were no sectors or professions that were not seriously affected, but all of those linked to the sea were hit particularly hard. It was a time in which the Brittany region, in which 60% of French fishermen resided, was going through great difficulties. Very few fishermen could earn enough to maintain their families at decent levels. The investigations directed by Fr. Lebret, from port to port, and published in his newspaper, reflected this extreme situation.

The situation was such that out of 85,000 fishermen identified in the census, it was found that there was work for only 30,000. As a consequence, 55,000 found themselves forced to emigrate. Fr. Lebret asked if this was good for France, and whether all of those unemployed could not have found a job in the public sector or in the factories in the industrial cities. Before giving in to the disaster, the first order of business was to urgently find financial aid, to guarantee a minimum income for each family. To do this required getting organized, creating a solid union in each branch of activity linked to the sea. The need was to assist the state in managing the fishing sector in Brittany.

A consideration of the circumstances led Fr. Lebret to favor a protectionist policy. He feared the social consequences of the laissez faire policy that the French government seemed to follow. He did not want to see French sailors forced to live on the miserable pay of the Portuguese fisherman of that time. He did not want to see them condemned to poverty by competition. He did not want to see his land decimated and deprived of its children. The storm needed to be weathered, and thus adequate measures were required.

Fr. Lebret's actions were carried out through the trade union, of which his close collaborator Ernest Lamort was the heart and soul. The interprofessional committees of the various branches of activity linked to fishing were of such effectiveness that he ended up calling them the greatest spontaneous organization that had ever existed in France. With his trade union activity solidly based on data, he sought nothing else than to save his people, to prevent the coast of Brittany from being transformed into a desert.

Before the end of the war, Fr. Lebret was already thinking of broadening and deepening the work begun in Saint-Malo. He intended to set up a center where more time was dedicated to field research and doctrinal study, without preventing his collaborators from taking responsibility for a sector where they could verify and corroborate their reflections. He wished to join economic questions and human ones. On September 24, 1941 in Marseilles, the *Economie et Humanisme* association was registered. His collaborators included Dominicans and laymen, such as the well-known economist Francois Perroux. A year later his celebrated "Manifesto" appeared. Conceived in a closed economy, and in a France divided into two, it already contained the intuitions and ideas that would be developed in later years, such as the rejection of an economy based on profit, a critique of a society that does not propose structural changes beyond social reformism, the distinction between goods and needs, and an initial formulation of a communitarian economy.

In this period in Marseilles, without abandoning his direct work with the fishermen, Fr. Lebret promoted research sessions. The center was soon moved to Lyons, which was considered more suitable to achieve better and broader circulation of the work done.

The year 1947 was decisive, for both Fr. Lebret and the *Economie et Humanisme* association. Invited by the Free School of Political Science of Sao Paulo, Brazil, Fr. Lebret taught a course from May to September and visited various countries in Latin America and the United States. His lectures aroused a great deal of interest. Those who participated realized that they were listening to a great master and a fraternal companion. And they were right: he was this indeed.

His time in Brazil and his travels to other Latin American countries made a profound impression on him. The condition of acute poverty of most of the population in those areas touched him so deeply that he decided to dedicate himself to helping the underdeveloped countries.

Upon returning to France, Fr. Lebret seemed to be almost a different man. He had discovered what the lack of development means through its most degrading manifestations, namely, hunger, shanties, illiteracy, infant mortality and the chronic lack of work. His contact with that stunning poverty, that was so widespread, made him say that the poorest Frenchman is rich, if compared to the people in Latin America.

Starting from this situation, we can speak of a new period in his life, when Fr. Lebret concentrated his attention on the social and economic problems of underdeveloped countries. Thus, in 1958, when he was totally convinced that development was the problem of the century, he founded the International Institute of Research for Training and Development (IRFED).

Like *Economie et Humanisme,* IRFED was also conceived to host a broad series of activities. First of all, it was a research center that aimed to define the conditions of harmonized development, meaning development that was not satisfied with mere economic growth, such as an increase of GDP, but was centered on the progress of peoples, fulfilling their lives as human beings. Therefore within the center Fr. Lebret created the "Development and Civilization" section, thus highlighting his mistrust of "economism" and his conviction that the battle for authentic development included the search for a new civilization that assumed the values of pre-industrial societies.
Furthermore, IRFED was a training institute that each year welcomed a hundred students of different ages and experiences, coming especially from Latin America, Africa, the Maghreb and the Middle East, but also Asia.

Fr. Lebret placed great stress on the question of training. He was absolutely convinced of the need to rely on good techniques in the economic, social and human disciplines, but he placed saw more value in the importance of being driven by respect and preferential love for these indigent peoples. He wanted his people to have a spirit of service; for them to be a sort of religious Congregation, as he said, a replication of the ancient Orders that dedicated themselves to the redemption of prisoners.

At this point in his life Fr. Lebret had now become a global authority. He was called on by various bishops in Latin America, Africa, and even Vietnam. He was an advisor to Senegal. From 1960 to 1964 he undertook a mission to Lebanon, a country he had come to know and love when he was young. This was his last great work. Previously he had occasionally gone to Rwanda and Venezuela. The Vatican sent him as a representative to various UN conferences.

We thus come to the last stage of Fr. Lebret's life, in which he would play an important role in the Vatican. During the course of his life his works and thinking were increasingly acknowledged. This earned him the admiration and trust of John XXIII and Cardinal Montini. In 1962 Fr. Lebret was appointed head of the Holy See's delegation to the United Nations Conference on the Application of Science and Technology for the Benefit of the Less Developed Areas, held in Geneva. His intervention can be considered a true testament. He masterfully traced the broad outlines of his central conception on harmonized development.

Fr. Lebret devoted the last four years of his service to directly serving the Church in Rome. He thought nothing could make more sense and be more valuable than this service. Those were years in which, through Vatican II, the Church was opening up to the world. Paul VI showed affectionate admiration for Fr. Lebret, and in 1964 named him a council expert. He was received in private audiences multiple times, and had the opportunity to express his point of view to the Pope on the expectations created by the announcement of the schema "The Church in the Modern World." In February 1965, he delivered the text of the chapter on the international community.

Unfortunately, during the last session of the Council, Fr. Lebret was gravely ill. He had been reduced to only a shadow of his former self. Paul VI himself recommended he not overtax himself. Schema XIII had given rise to *Gaudium et Spes*. Fr. Lebret cultivated the idea of establishing a Secretariat for Justice, a hope expressed in the document. He felt that it should have a doctrinal function, given that, as Paul VI had also written, development was the new name for peace. The most crucial task of that Secretariat would be to define a coherent doctrine of integral and harmonized development. In addition, it would promote actions to transform that doctrine into reality.

Fr. Lebret died on July 20, 1966, before this project was carried out. The year after his death *Populorum Progressio* appeared, in which he was expressly cited by Paul VI., Fr. Lebret's influence on the preparation of this fundamental document can be detected in almost every paragraph.

For those who had become familiar with his written works, his way of expressing himself and his vocabulary, it was very easy to recognize not only his inspiration, but also entire sentences quoted from him. From his diary, we known when and how Paul VI asked for his collaboration for the Encyclical. So, it is no surprise that the Pope himself said he felt veneration and devotion for Fr. Lebret, and that the Encyclical on the development of peoples was a homage to his memory, recalling this great man of the Church.

His thought

We have already examined Fr. Lebret's thinking to a significant extent by describing the various stages of his life. Thus it will suffice to stress three points of his philosophy: *1)* his view of the common good; *2)* his critique of liberalism and Marxism; and *3)* his conception of harmonized development.

For Fr. Lebret, the common good is the good of a human society. Its members seek the good, realize the good, and all receive it together. There is a common desire for the good, and it is obtained by virtue of social justice. Each of us is incapable of finding our own good by ourselves: we need help. It is written in our nature that we need others to be able to reach our own perfection.

Each person must serve the common good. Therefore, the rich must in some manner make their goods available to others; the wise must communicate the truth; and those who have more talents must help others. Thus, property is in relation to the common good. For Fr. Lebret, disorder arises when advantageous situations (lands, factories, science, abilities) are used for their own purposes. In his view, this is what modern capitalism has done: it has not placed itself at the service of the common good, but betrayed it. With its free competition, capitalism creates a social structure that is contrary to social justice. It favors the one who is less human and less honest, who abuses his employees, making them work as long as possible for the lowest salary, and with the help of misleading advertising, lowers prices and takes over the market. An essential condition for the common good is general prosperity and mutual trust. This requires profound education, that is, a religious education. It follows that the Church has an necessary role in achieving the common good.

Despite being driven by this great humanitarian ideal, Fr. Lebret firmly opposed Marxism. He had read *Capital*, and as a result, he understood that the tenets of Marxism were very far from the doctrine of the common good. So, he rejected it, based on his Christian anthropology, as an almost determinist system, in which there is no place for the notion of the person, for the exercise of liberty, and thus for morality. He considered it not less harmful than capitalism, the other side of the same coin.

Fr. Lebret fought vigorously for a new civilization: this was his proposal. To understand it, we need to start from his idea that development includes much more than economic growth. It goes far beyond an increase of GDP. Furthermore, development that is limited to succeeding in increasing production, would not be true development.

Fr. Lebret deduced the notion of development from a well-known reality: that of a plant, an animal or a person who grows. It involves an internal equilibrium that is maintained during growth. It is a harmony that belongs to the being's nature in development. This shows the value of the being; it is the evolution of its potential towards the condition that realizes it. As a consequence, it is advancing towards the optimum, and concludes when this has been reached. But for the human person the optimal conditions follow each other. There is that of nurture, of strength, active abilities, intellectual maturity, and the fullness of moral and spiritual life.

Our aspirations are met only with this organic conception of development. It is orderly growth, analogous to that of living beings. It greatly transcends the economic dimension. It deals with broader human questions, since it includes expressions like economic, social and cultural development, and so forth.

For Fr. Lebret the essential issue, in both developed and underdeveloped countries, was that of creating a civilization based on solidarity. He was worried about the impact of Western industrial civilization on the values of traditional civilizations. The development of the Third World should not consist of economic growth that made peoples lose their identity, their soul and the reasons to live. Fr. Lebret understood that in preserving traditional values there was the risk of rejecting development, but also that destroying those values through industrial civilization meant abandoning oneself. What to do? How to get out of this impasse? Fr. Lebret's response was that the solution lies in a symbiosis of value systems. When this occurs, development is much more than elevating the global levels of production that is poorly distributed: it is a dynamic harmonizing of previous values and new values, of autochthonous values and imported values. This harmonized development is characterized by the realization of an economy as human as possible in a system of true solidarity.

His spirituality

In considering how occupied Fr. Lebret was with temporal questions, some are surprised that he was a Dominican. He responded to this objection himself, saying that if he had not been a sailor first, and then a Dominican, he could not have carried out all of his works.

It all started in his birthplace of Brittany, to which he always felt a deep connection. In his infancy and within his family he began to appreciate the values so typical of the Bretons. Not a few of them were men of faith, bearing the signs of hard work in the fields and at sea, with an enterprising spirit, capable of sacrifice. When he returned to Saint-Malo after becoming a Dominican, he found a Brittany demoralized by the economic and social crisis of the 1930s. Before him he saw poverty, at times almost misery, and the insecurity of many who were faced with the prospect of having to emigrate. It was not just the fishermen: the farmers also saw no future in their land. It is estimated that between 1900 and 1940 approximately 600,000 Bretons had to emigrate. This reality, seeing Brittany lacking authentic development, began to orient Fr. Lebrets' life. He felt that his vocation called on him to work courageously for his people, for his Bretons.

Educated in an environment full of faith where he developed his love for God, from a young age he wished to be a priest. He had thought of entering the Trappist monastery of Briquebecq, near Cherbourg, but he soon recognized that his temperament was more active. In Lebanon, he went on a vocational retreat with the Jesuits, but they told him he was too independent to be a child of St. Ignatius and suggested he become a Dominican. Jokingly, he would say that the Jesuits decided they did not want him. This event was providential, because Fr. Lebret passionately loved the Order of Preachers. When he was in Itly, he did everything possible to celebrate the Eucharist on the tomb of St. Dominic in Bologna. In his diary, we can read of the emotion this provoked in him.

Fr. Lebret intensely loved the spirit of his Order, and recognized St. Thomas as his intellectual master. He liked the regular life of the convent, with its times for prayer, silence and work, as it enriched him and helped him in his mission. In this regard, it should be said that Fr. Lebret was a man of prayer and contemplation. In addition, he left us an important spiritual work of eight volumes. He had a decisive influence on the life of many believers, offering them an engaged spirituality.

Indeed, when we read his writings, some aspects recur: an intense life of communion with the Lord, that he expresses in prayer, with unabashed candor, always youthful in his enthusiasm for his Lord, whom he trusts with the soul of a child. Strictly linked to this contemplative dimension, to this adoring gaze on his God, is the loving, sweet gaze that he focuses on all the creatures God loves. This merciful love for his neighbor allowed him no rest in the search for the common good, in the promotion of universal brotherhood. Love pushed him to fight against all injustice: a battle that he would carry forward for his entire life.

The prayers that Fr. Lebret composed are the result of contemplation, of a mysticism infused with flesh and blood. There is no impression of a flight to the spiritual; there is nothing that hurts the feelings of those who believe in the urgency of taking root in history here and now.

In 1946 and 1949 Fr. Lebret was in Rome, at the church of San Luigi, where he preached some spiritual exercises, that were then put into writing and published. He went over the history of salvation and reached the conclusion that we Christians are responsible for our neighbors, but that by now our neighbors are all the people, humanity as a whole. Thus, when he reads the parable of the rich man and Lazarus in the Gospel (*Lk* 16,19-31), he immediately places it in our history: Lazarus, today, is most of humanity.

"We have become the evil rich man. Lazarus is crouched down under our table and must settle for the crumbs that fall: one-hundredths, two-hundredths, one-thousandth of our national incomes [...]. Lazarus is legion, the immense majority of humanity. Lazarus was once far away, overseas. Our economic system exploited him frenetically. Today Lazarus is close, the world has gotten smaller. Lazarus begins to exist for us, we have just discovered him. Judging from our newspapers, he has taken a large place in the life of the world. We do not love him anymore, we fear him. Lazarus has learned to revolt… he learns to read and react… he threatens our safety, our peace. We could help Lazarus much more, but to do this, the great peoples who are economically powerful would need to cease hating and spending for their defense or to attack others about thirty times what they spend to assist populations in misery. Lazarus is exasperated due to our pride and our stupidity."

Fr. Lebret was undoubtedly very much loved and sought after, just as he also loved much. In conclusion of these considerations we provide a prayer of his, entitled *Those who in you I loved, Lord*: "My God, I believe I have loved many things, in you, along my path. / I understand that it has always been too little, but I understand that it was the best of my life so full of selfishness. / When, as a child, I loved that poor neighbor who did not have a dress to go to Mass. / I loved the beggars who took a sack from house to house to fill it with bread. / I loved the dockhands of Port Said, with whom we loaded coal onto our boat. / I loved the Germans, whose fleet we had just destroyed, and who called desperately in the thick fog among the banks of Flanders. / I loved the fishermen who fled towards the city, reduced to hunger by mechanization and the global crisis. / I loved the inhabitants of the hovels of Marseilles to whom Father Loew took me. / I loved the blacks of the *favelas* of Rio and the *mocambos* of Recife… I loved the garbage men of Tokyo whose miserable dwellings were destroyed by the police… I loved so many wretches that I do not remember the number… / I loved the rich, slaves to their wealth… the politicians who had neither the competence nor the greatness to properly fulfill their duty. / I loved all sorts of men, many miserable poor who could only be raised up by the testimony of authentic love. / My God, I did too little for these men who I loved in you, and for all there was in them of valor and hope. / Nevertheless, may my distress seize also all those who still bear your name and who, by joining their forces, could make the world a better place."

Conclusion

We believe it is very appropriate to encourage the study of the complete works of Fr. Lebret, so he will become known and much can be learned from him. This Breton – and as such, a man of great mettle – took the social problems of his native region, his country and the world very seriously. We owe largely to him the introduction of the entire theme of development in the Social Doctrine of the Church.

He was ahead of his time with his conception of what authentic development is, i.e. the development of the human person as a whole and of all people. In his time – the 1950s and 1960s – the nascent theory of development was very limited, largely to economic factors. When we read his writings, we cannot but admire the clarity and relevance of his thought. There everything is born from his profound spirituality, from seeing himself obliged to take social action because he was touched by divine mercy. His great legacy deserves recognition and admiration.

Mysticism without God

Giandomenico Mucci, SJ

"Mysticism presents itself as the space where a speculative study of religious facts meets the need to live religious experience in the milieu of the advanced secularism of western society."[1]

The men and women of our secularized society still live under the action and sign of *rasonnierende ffenlichkeit* (public reasoning) of Kantian memory, which makes the truth the result of a rational, discursive and collective work of the whole of humanity. This does not mean that this culture of formal rationality, typical of the Enlightenment, is not today undermined by the return of the irrational and of individualism, or by the natural tendency of man toward the magic sense of things and to symbolic function. This is how secular analysts explain the current interest in mysticism.

Not being able to accept as true the interpretation which Catholic theology gives of mysticism, they explain the mystical experience as a reaction to the crisis of culture derived from the Enlightenment: a simplistic reaction of those who want to overcome the opposition between religious experience and reason, perhaps after struggling with it themselves. "If postmodernity, as the time of the end of the Enlightenment myths, is witnessing the return of the religious and new demand for meaning, it is also undergoing the charm of those spiritual realities that

---

1. Mucci, G., "La mistica come crocevia del postmoderno", in ID., *I cattolici nella temperie del relativismo*, Milan: Jaca Book, 2005, p.371.

express the desire for creativity and self-discovery beyond the disappointments and failures attributed to reason."[2]

It was Norberto Bobbio who recognized that "because the great answers are beyond the reach of our mind, man remains a religious being, despite all the demythologizing processes of secularization, all the claims of the death of God that characterize the modern age and even more so the contemporary age."[3]

An exhumation

Clearly, these facts and considerations are not considered as sufficient proof by the Union of Atheists and Rationalist Agnostics. They have published a work by Fritz Mauthner (1849-1923), whose first German edition, in 4 hefty volumes, dates back to the years 1920-1923: *Atheism and its History in the West*. It certainly is a minor work in the history of philosophy. It is, however, entitled to a place both for its dependency on the thought of Ernst Mach, a contemporary of Mauthner, and for the influence that it exercised on the thinking of Ludwig Wittgenstein as well as on the analytic philosophy of language and on the art of Hugo von Hofmannsthal. It seems to us that its publication in Italian was done not to fill a lacuna in the history of philosophy but rather as a catalyst to reignite the languishing discussion on atheism.

This work of Mauthner stands together with another of his works, *Contributions to a Critique of Language*, first published in German in 3 volumes from 1901 to 1903. In light of the empirical theory of knowledge, Mauthner denies language the possibility of knowing reality. He posits that language is purely conventional and equates language and thought while proposing that the superseding of language is represented as redemption from the "superstition of the Word" by means of a "mysticism without words." Since reality is always mediated and

---

2. Ib., 373.
3. Cfr D. Antiseri, "La riscoperta della fede nel nuovo secolo", in *Il Tempo*, April 15, 2001, 1.

limited by the use of language, only "a mystic contemplation" could capture the true essence of the world.

This linguistic criticism leads to the senselessness of any statement about God. The history of atheism is the history of the concept of God and, given the premise, it is also the story of free thought that has evolved and interweaved with the history of unbelief, heresy and philosophy. For Mauthner, criticism of theism is born from the criticism of language, which also is. If the criticism of language lowers the words to "images of images of images," each god is a verbal god that can be demolished. The history of atheism documents the effort to overthrow the supreme Name that recapitulates all the forms of verbal idolatry and to free man from psychological and political subjugation to the power of the Church.[4]

It is a little ironic that an author who wrote seven large volumes on the fallacies and fatuousness of language, with all this entails, was clearly not able to free himself from language. As for mysticism without words, a theory which purports to establish that language and God are nonsensical, it might be possible to recover the concept. referring it only to language and limiting it to the poetic world. As a verse by Pascoli suggests, "Dreaming is the infinite shadow of Truth." In a dream, we can experiment with what words never satiate which is thirst for knowledge and truth. It remains the case that Christian mysticism is something other than a dream.

Mysticism and Atheism

Among many definitions or descriptions of mysticism, we favor that of Saint Thomas, who refers to Christian mysticism as: "The knowledge of God's will or goodness, knowledge that is effective and experimental, when a man experiences in himself the taste of God's sweetness and pleasure in God's divine

---

4. P. Kampits, "Mauthner, Fritz", in F. Volpi (ed.), *Dizionario delle opere filosofiche*, Milan: Mondadori, 2000, 734f; G. Vitiello, "La mistica senza Dio di Fritz Mauthner", in *Corriere della Sera*, "La Lettura", July 8, 2012, 16.

will."⁵ This is the definition of an experience of "unity," of an experience that the human spirit has of the Absolute in the time of this present life.⁶ If that is how it is interpreted – and this is how it should be interpreted in its Trinitarian and Christological aspect – is it perhaps possible to think that Christian mysticism is a yeast for the contemporary world? We think not.

The current rebirth of religiousness should not deceive us. It is true that nowadays, the acceptance of religious phenomena is widespread, from those that retrieve ancient traditions to those of a more fundamentalist brand. But in a society and a culture of crisis, these are explainable as the search for the final meaning of reality and of life. When they are not external and emotional phenomena, they betray their own superficiality in the eyes of those who consider the existing gap between the declared Christian faith and the practices of Christian morality. "As in the far gone Alexandrian age, at the sunset of the Hellenistic civilization and with it of the ancient world, we see a turgid religious phenomenon where improper forms of religiosity and syncretism are interwoven with authentic religious experiences and sometimes they coexist in the same person."⁷

So it is an exaggeration to speak of mysticism in this context. Rather, it seems to revive the theory made famous by Rudolf Otto according to which the divine and the religious can be grasped not with rationally lucid concepts, but with irrational and sentimental skills that man feels when he sinks below his humanity. That is when he rebels and yearns for the *mysterium* dwelling above him.⁸ Our current age is precisely the epoch of the science of language, of phenomenologies, of herme-

---

5. *Sum. Theol.*, II-II, q.97, a. 2, ad 2um. *Est cognitio divinae bonitatis vel voluntatis affectiva seu experimentalis, dum quis experitur in seipso gustum divinae dulcedinis et complacentiam divinae voluntatis.*

6. Cfr M. Vannini, *Il volto del Dio nascosto. L'esperienza mistica dall'Iliade a Simone Weil*, Milan, Mondadori, 1999, 17.

7. A. Rigobello, "Perche si torna a parlare di Dio?", in *Oss. Rom.*, September 30, 1992, 3.

8. A. Ghisalberti, "La mistica cristiana continua ad affascinare", in *Vita e Pensiero* 93 (2010) 122.

neutics that seem hit by shortages of expression only when philosophical discourse must address the question or the problem of God. It is the era of agnosticism and still, in many ways, of atheism, which lives undetected with the concerns raised by the search for meaning. However, it is possible that the agnostic or even the atheist, while failing to escape from an exclusively worldly perspective, may live a "spirituality" which in the believer amounts to a tacit invocation of the heart.[9] And this echoes the paradoxical prayers of Hemingway, of Zinoviev and Caproni, which give grounds for Wittgenstein writing, "To pray is to think about the meaning of life."[10] It is mysticism without God. This is how Rossana Rossanda and Sergio Quinctius saw it, one ascribing it to irrationalism, the other to aestheticizing syncretism, both concerning the immanent concept of human life.

In all this, however, there is a positive fact. Religious experience, at least, the idea and the desire for religious experience, are not dead things. The civilization that has arisen knows in its own way its own religiosity, complex, subjective, personal, tormented, capable of impulse and closure, fluid, but not to the point of declaring the presence and significance of Christianity outdated. For its part, the Christian always hopes that the Lord "will give to all the possibility of being made partners, in a way known to God, with the paschal mystery."[11] But mysticism is something else.

The Youth

The natural vocation of young Europeans to the religious experience has been noticed. They live in uncertainty and insecurity: the experience gives them stability. They live without

---

9. Cfr T. Goffi, "Ateo", in S. De Fiores - T. Goffi, (eds), *Nuovo Dizionario di Spiritualita*, Cinisello Balsamo, Milan, Paoline, 1985, 108f.

10. G. Ravasi, "La preghiera, respiro dell'anima", in *Il Sole 24 Ore*, December 30, 2012, 28; S. Acquaviva, "Cercando un altro Dio nel crepuscolo degli dei", in *Corriere della Sera*, July 22, 1992, 9.

11. Second Vatican Council, *Gaudium et Spes*, n.22e.

a past and do not see a future: this experience promises them a tradition, a history, eternity. They live, dissatisfied, in a state of confusion: this experience gives them a norm. They inhabit an earth disfigured by man: religious experience is beauty. There are many young people who silently experience this attraction. And it is a meeting and a clash: experience, adhesion, rejection, anger.[12]

The tendency to mysticism seems a characteristic feature of many young people, especially those who come from higher socio-cultural strata. This is demonstrated by the proliferation of mystic youth movements of an irrational and esoteric orientation. In the 1970s the Jesus Movement appeared in the Anglo-Saxon world. In this movement many young people committed to stay away from the temptations of sex and drugs and emotionally gathered around the figure of Jesus. Other young people were fascinated by the passive doctrines found in Eastern religions. The phenomenon remains a witness to the need for religious experience and "mysticism" that in the past exercised its influence on the Catholic youth.

Such a need, in debt to para-religious irrationalism, may have had its genesis in the reaction to the rationalization of urban-industrial society and, at least partially, to the apparent or real bureaucratization of historical religious organizations. In any case, genuine Christian mysticism is something else and grows, by divine grace, within the faith of the Church in a climate of ascetism and prayer, for it is experience of the transcendent.[13]

This means that authentic Christian mysticism participates in the simplicity of God; it is not mixed with the often sinful ambiguity of earthly existence. It is not born as a product of a culture in which the sacred and cosmic, the sacred and erotic, sacred, esoteric and demonic, fanaticism, magic and

---

12. Cfr M. Ventura, "I giovani europei chiedono di credere", in *Corriere della Sera*, "La lettura", September 9, 2012, 7.
13. Cfr P.G. Grasso, "Giovani", in S. De Fiores-T. Goffi (eds), *Nuovo Dizionario di Spiritualita*, cit., 740f.

superstition, are mixed up. These are so often the characteristics by which a mysticism without God can be recognized.[14]

Benedict XVI, during a homily, exhorted Christians to remain near Jesus without fear, to let themselves be purified of the dross that compromises our spiritual relationship with the Lord and with others. He quoted one of Origen's homilies where this ancient Church Father referenced an expression attributed to Jesus, probably authentic, even if it is not contained in Sacred Scripture: "Whoever is near me is near fire."[15] A text that lends itself well to describing Christian mysticism.

So too a poem by Dylan Thomas expresses allegorically the nostalgia that many of our contemporaries have:

> Being but men, we walked into the trees
> Afraid, letting our syllables be soft
> For fear of waking the rooks,
> For fear of coming
> Noiselessly into a world of wings and cries.
>
> If we were children we might climb,
> Catch the rooks sleeping, and break no twig,
> And, after the soft ascent,
> Thrust out our heads above the branches
> To wonder at the unfailing stars.
> Out of confusion, as the way is,
> And the wonder, that man knows,
> Out of the chaos would come bliss.
>
> That, then, is loveliness, we said,
> Children in wonder watching the stars,
> Is the aim and the end.
> Being but men we walked into the trees, afraid.

---

14. Cfr G.F. Zuanazzi, "Patologia spirituale", ib., 1164-1166.
15. Cfr *Oss. Rom.*, May 24-25, 2010, 8.

The World of Almodovar

Virgilio Fantuzzi, SJ

Julieta (Emma Suarez) lives in Madrid with her daughter Antia (Blanca Pares). Both suffer in silence over the loss of Xoan (Daniel Grao), father of Antia and husband of Julieta. But sometimes pain divides people, instead of uniting them. On the day Antia turns eighteen years old, she abandons her mother without giving her any explanation. Julieta starts searching for Antia by all means available, but the only thing she manages to discover is how little she knows about her daughter.

A mother's heart

The film *Julieta* by Pedro Almodovar examines a mother's fight to survive uncertainty. Little by little, she comes to understand why her daughter decided to erase her from her own life. The film debuted at the Cannes Film Festival 2016 and talks about destiny, about guilt, and about the unfathomable mystery which pushes some to abandon the people they love – to ignore them as if they had never meant anything, as if they had never existed.

The folds of red fabric on which the opening credits appear might recall a stage curtain, ready to be lifted in order to start the dramatic action. But the red fabric, as later shown by a wider image, is that of Julieta's red dress, behind which beats a mother's wounded heart.

The second object to appear on-screen is a terracotta sculpture depicting a seated man. Julieta carefully folds protective wrapping around the statuette and places it, together with other objects, into a cardboard box. The year is 2016, and Julieta is packing her bags with the intention of definitively leaving Madrid and moving to Portugal.

The sculpture was made by Ava (Inma Custa), Julieta's artist friend, who loved to listen, as she molded terracotta statues, to the ancient myths recounted by Julieta, a professor of classical literature.

"The gods created men and other beings with the help of clay and fire...", says Julieta. It is 1985. The young Julieta is played by Adriana Ugarte, who is some thirty years younger than Emma Suarez. The two women are both splendid, as well as alike, despite the difference in age.

The women's relationship with the sculpture, in the symbolic language weaving its way through the film's imagery, is an allusion to the power of women, a theme which is dear to Almodovar. "The woman," says the director, "not only gives life, but she is stronger in fighting, administering, suffering and enjoying all that life brings with it. Only fate is stronger than her."

A deadly silence

Antia, daughter of Julieta and Xoan, turns 18 in 2003. Now an adult, she decides to go and spend three months on retreat in the Aragonese Pyrenees. Never having been separated from her before, Julieta is distressed by the idea of her daughter's departure.

The mother watches her daughter disappear as she walks down the stairs of their home. She tries to hide her pain as best she can. The situation reminds her of previous goodbyes she has endured, of which she has never spoken to her daughter. One of those goodbyes took place on a train during an overnight journey in 1985, the same night Antia was conceived.

A man had sat down opposite Julieta with tears in his eyes, and had tried to start a conversation. She had responded coldly, and had never been able to forget the man's gaze.

The other gaze which still torments her is the gaze of Xoan, the fisherman she had met that same night on the train. Julieta and Xoan had started a family and had gone to live in Redes, a fishing village in Galicia. One day, thirteen years later, they had had an argument about Xoan's past – something Julieta had discovered, which had badly disappointed her. She had decided to go outside. Xoan had begged her to stay and talk, but she had taken refuge in silence, and had left the house.

Xoan had watched her walk out the door, disoriented and a little beseeching. Julieta had returned home that evening intending to resume their interrupted conversation, but Xoan was not there, and they never had the opportunity to finish that conversation. Shortly after she had left, Xoan had gone fishing and that afternoon a sudden and violent storm ended his life.

After receiving no word of her daughter for years, Julieta destroys all physical reminders which connect her to Antia, and moves to a different address. She decides to bury her daughter's memory. Nothing must remind her of Antia. She goes to live in an anonymous apartment in the suburbs, far from the city center where she had lived with her daughter.

Among the symbolic elements of this film is the furnishing of Julieta's various homes, marking the different phases of her life. From the fisherman's house in Galicia, its windows facing the sea – sometimes dazzling with color, at other times black with the storm – to the old-style house in the heart of Madrid where she moves with Antia, who wanted to live near her inseparable friend Bea (Michelle Jenner). The suburban apartment with its white walls and lack of ornaments that reflect the emptiness inside Julieta.

When she decides to leave Madrid, never to return (we watched her pack her boxes for the move), a fortuitous encounter with Bea, who she hasn't seen for years, causes Julieta to suddenly change her plans. Bea says she bumped into Antia by chance on Lake Como, and told her that her mother still lives in Madrid.

The news Julieta receives from Bea is scant (Antia is married, she has three children...), but enough to radically change her plans. She breaks off the relationship with her new partner Lorenzo (Dario Grandinetti) without providing any explanation – one of the succession of silences unfolding throughout the film. She returns to the building where she had shared an apartment with her daughter, and attempts to resume contact with her ghost, writing a long letter in which she says everything she had never said when they lived together.

In 2016 Julieta walks around the places she used to stroll through with her daughter in 1998, after they moved to Madrid. She wanders the streets of the same neighborhood, she stops at the basketball court to which she used to bring Antia with her friend Bea... One imagines Almodovar, just like Julieta, is trying to set his time machine in motion by revisiting the places where, from the start of the 1980s, he began to direct his first films. His reverie is not hard to follow...

Labyrinths

Labyrinth of Passion (*Laberinto de pasiones*, 1982) is a fairy tale, of sorts. Evil witch Toraya (Helga Line) causes a rift between two preadolescents, Riza Niro (Imanol Arias) and Sexilia (Cecilia Roth), who love each other without malice. The trauma caused by this negative experience pushes them both to take wrong turns. He finds himself a homosexual, she finds herself a nymphomaniac.

We catch up with them years later in the nightclubs of Madrid, where the *movida* is in full swing. Neither of them are able to find their place. But their winding paths, full of unforeseen twists and identity swaps, are precisely what will lead them to meet again, help them to remove the inhibitions created by their old trauma, and return them to the firm ground of a harmonious relationship.

The film contains a very colorful re-enactment of Madrid's nightlife at the start of the 80s, which Almodovar himself helped to animate as an eclectic showman, combining pop, rock and funk experiences. The director, who was then beginning what would turn out to be his dazzling career, sowed dismay among right-thinking citizens, allowing himself freedoms – depicting coarse situations, using vulgar language – which had long been repressed by the official conformism of Franco's Spain.

Dark Habits (*Entre tinieblas*, 1983) is a film which irritated the public and the critics, both for its irreverent content (a small, female monastery illustrated more in light of its human weaknesses than its religious virtues) and for the manner of its filming, which was considered unsophisticated, inclined to a certain carelessness, and not without aggressiveness towards the spectator (all that vomiting into the camera…).

Almodovar refutes the accusation of anticlericalism, saying that religion, for him, consists in looking people in the eye with compassion when they live in difficulty, and particularly when they are women, more vulnerable than men to suffering harassment of all kinds – whether they are women pushed to the margins of society, forced to perform the most humiliating roles to survive, or whether they are religious women confined to the restrictive spaces of a monastery, where it is not easy to maintain the balance between the limitations imposed by its rules and the surge of unbridled impulses.

Almodovar, inclined to metaphor, adds to the monastery a young tiger, taken in by the nuns when he was a cub, and cossetted as if he were their own child. Now the tiger is three years old. Fed with meat even when the nuns are fasting, he knows what he wants and how to get it.

Law of Desire (*La ley del deseo*, 1987) is a real melodrama of masculinity. Pablo (Eusebio Poncela), a successful screenwriter and director, is in love with Juan (Miguel Molina), but is not averse to other adventures, and begins a relationship with Antonio (Antonio Banderas). The latter wants Pablo all to himself and kills Juan. Pablo is devastated. The affair has a tragic ending.

According to Almodovar, romantic passion cannot be controlled, whether it is homosexual or heterosexual. However, no one assures the victims of this passion that they will find a soulmate with whom to share it. This is the common fate of Pablo and Antonio, both in love, but unrequited.

The character of Pablo, who is a cinema and theatre director as well as a writer, allows Almodovar to insert metalinguistic passages into his story, including for example a staging of the female monologue *La Voix Humaine* by Cocteau, performed by Tina (Carmen Maura), Pablo's transsexual sister. Also performing onstage is Ada (Manuela Velasco), a young girl whom Tina looks after as a mother, singing in play-back *Ne me quitte pas* by Jacques Brel, recorded by Marisa Matarazzo.

Both Cocteau's lyrics and Brel's song lend musical voice to Almodovar's beloved theme of passion's destructive force. The show within the show also marks the failure of Pablo, who is unable, as a director, to sublimate his romantic sufferings into art.

When he is involved in a traffic accident which causes temporary loss of memory, Pablo is able to establish a relationship with Tina, from whom he learns his family's secrets – aspects of reality he did not know, which he must begin to deal with from now onwards.

Cover models

Women on the Verge of a Nervous Breakdown (*Mujeres al borde de un ataque de nervios, 1987*) opens with a fanciful title sequence, inspired by the graphics of women's magazines and 1960s posters. Hair spray, heavy lipstick, and conventional "cover girl" imagery set the stage for the appearance of Pepa (Carmen Maura), an actress who works in television and is currently employed in the dubbing of an American film.

She is the woman on the verge of a nervous breakdown. As she is about to be abandoned by her live-in lover Ivan (Fernando Guillen), also an actor and involved in dubbing the same film, Pepa realizes she is pregnant. She would like to tell Ivan, but is unable to contact him.

The film finds her in a deep slumber, provoked by the substantial doses of sleeping pills she takes. She fails to be woken by the half dozen alarm clocks which surround her bed. She will be late to work. She dreams in black and white that Ivan is busy flirting with every woman he meets in the street, whispering a film-worthy line to each one.

In the dubbing room, a camera rolls. Technical details on the mechanism which produces artificial dreams. Pepa and Ivan separately dub Joan Crawford and Sterling Hayden in a fiery western by Nicholas Ray (*Johnny Guitar*, 1954). Life and cinema are out of synch. The telephone complicates matters – instead of bringing the parties closer, it creates new barriers with the intervention of the answering machine.

With the story thus set in motion, there is nothing to be done but proceed at its ever-increasing pace, from one plot twist to the next, as if it were a clockwork ballet. The enterprising Pepa, always in action, is presented in counterpoint to other women, played by the actresses Julieta Serrano, Rossy de Palma, Maria Barranco, Kiti Manver, and Loles Leon, all dressed up to the nines in high heels, fishnet stockings, tight skirts, flashy jewelry, odd little hats...

Each time Pepa is about to make contact with Ivan, something unexpected happens. In the end, knowing he is in danger because one of his exes has gone crazy and is trying to kill him, she manages to reach him and save his life. Having seen him again, however, she decides to let him go, keeping her secret and her child to herself.

In *The Flower of my Secret* (*La flor de mi secreto*, 1993) Leocadia, known as Leo (Marisa Paredes), writes romantic fiction under the pseudonym Amanda Gris, but privately is tormented by the failure of her marriage. She is madly in love with her husband Paco (Imanol Arias), a NATO official always on mission, whom she misses like crazy. But Paco shows little interest in her. He is in love with another woman, the psychologist Betty (Carme Elias), Leo's close friend and only confidante. The latter finds out the bitter truth through a series of plot twists, which go hand in hand with the misunderstandings created by the false identity behind which she conceals her literary activities.

Thus depression, attempted suicide, and last-minute rescue at the hands of Leo's mother, an elderly countrywoman who hates the chaotic life of Madrid, and removes her daughter to the fresh air of their hometown so that she can recover.

Leo's story — which finds a happy ending in the flowering of a new love between the writer and Angel (Juan Echanove), a journalist who edits the literary section of *El Pais* — is entwined with the story of Blanca (Manuela Vargas), a waitress who is passionate about flamenco. Her son Antonio (Joaquin Cortes), a penniless dancer and choreographer, having stolen the manuscript of a novel which Leo had binned as unpublishable, has managed to sell it to director Bigas Luna, who wants to make a film of it. With his earnings, Antonio has put together a show in which he dances with his mother to reveal extraordinary artistic talent — proof of the fact that life always has some happy surprise in store for those who do not give in to dismay, and trust in the future.

From comedy to drama

All About my Mother (*Todo sobre mi madre*, 1999). Manuela (Cecilia Roth), a nurse who deals with transplants, loses her eighteen-year-old son Esteban (Eloy Azorin) in an accident. The boy dies after being run over by a car while chasing Huma Rojo (Marisa Paredes), an actress starring in a performance of the play *A Streetcar Named Desire,* by Tennessee Williams. After the tragedy, Manuela decides to return to her hometown of Barcelona, to bring news of her son's death to her ex-husband Esteban, a transvestite who goes by the name of Lola (Toni Canto).

Manuela's arrival in Barcelona is spectacular. The city, dominated by the spires of the Sagrada Familia, conveys an idea of paradise from above. Immediately afterwards, the taxi which takes Manuela from the airport to the hotel passes through a sort of infernal bedlam. Sex and drugs are sold while transvestites, transsexuals, and other dubious characters work alongside "normal" prostitutes, in a jumble which some critics call Fellini-like, but more appropriately might be labelled Bosch-like.

Here Manuela meets Agrado (Antonia San Juan), an old friend, who saves her from a dangerous attack. Agrado puts Manuela in contact with Sister Rosa (Penelope Cruz), a young nun involved in social work, who can put her in touch with Lola.

Later in the film, which is inclined towards melodrama and not lacking in plot twists, Manuela, accompanied by Agrado, meets the actress Huma, who is romantically involved with her assistant Nina (Candela Pena). They create a quartet which allows for multiple role swaps.

Meanwhile, we find out that Sister Rosa is pregnant with Lola's child (Lola who was once Esteban, father of the young Esteban who died). Lola, having contracted HIV/AIDS, has also given it to Rosa. Rosa's family, whose conformism is stigmatized throughout the film by its pitiless description, is unable to take care of her. Assisted by Manuela and Agrado, Rosa dies in childbirth. Her boy (the third Esteban) is born needing special treatment to cure the illness inherited from his father.

Manuela adopts the child. Thus, she is returned to motherhood. During Rosa's funeral, the first Esteban (now Lola) reappears, in the guise of the angel of death. His terminal illness is consuming him little by little. He barely has time to be reconciled with the past before bidding his farewell to life. The youngest Esteban responds positively to treatment and eliminates any traces of previous infection from his body.

Thus, summarized, the film's plot might seem redundant and baroque. The story is rendered convincing by the sobriety of its style. They say that in the catalogue of human suffering there is nothing comparable to the pain of a mother at the loss of a child. During the filming of *All About My Mother*, Almodovar never ceased repeating to actress Cecilia Roth: "Cry as little as possible. Keep your tone of voice low." And to the other actresses, too, he said: "Dry, dry, dry…"

The key phrase of this film is taken from a line of the play *A Streetcar Named Desire*, where one of the characters (Blanche Dubois) says that she has faith in the kindness of strangers. Solidarity among women is the central theme. Mutual help is offered spontaneously by women who live in hardship. Manuela, who suffers most of all, is the one who most strives to help others.

The living and the dead

Talk to Her (*Hable con ella*, 2002). Always looking for the extreme, this time Almodovar comes across the unmoving, but still living, bodies of two women in a coma. Two pairs of characters (one male, one female) experience situations proceeding along parallel courses, but in opposite directions. The two women, because of traumatic accidents, lie suspended between life and death. The two men who look after them, connected to them by intense ties of affection, meet in the corridors of the hospital where the women have been admitted to neighboring rooms.

One of the two men, Benigno (Javier Camara), speaks to his woman, Alicia (Leonor Watling), convinced that she can hear and understand everything he says. The other man, Marco (Dario Grandinetti), cannot find the right words to express his feelings when faced with the body of his beloved Lydia (Rosario Flores), who is incapable of responding. Alicia, the woman to whom Benigno speaks, comes out of her coma and survives. Lydia, the one to whom Marco does not speak, dies.

Terrible things happen in this film. Benigno, who works as a nurse in the hospital and is a little weak in the mind, is seized by a moment of madness and impregnates Alicia. The child is born dead before its mother awakes, while Benigno pays for his offence with jail, where he commits suicide without ever learning that Alicia has awoken.

It is important to recognize the delicacy with which Almodovar tackles his difficult themes, and the effort he makes to elevate his narration to a higher register of expression – using, among other things, the contribution of exceptional collaborators such as choreographer Pina Bausch and musician Caetano Veloso (woven into the fabric of the film with brief cameos of the iconic roles they play in real life), and including his protégé Geraldine Chaplin in the cast.

Bad Education

In *Bad Education* (2004) the story follows three interconnected, parallel timelines.

1980. Film director Enrique Godel (Fele Martinez) receives a visit from former boarding school friend Ignacio (Gael Garcia Bernal), who says that he is an actor and that his stage name is Angel. Enrique struggles to recognize him. In reality, Ignacio/Angel is Juan, younger brother of the real Ignacio, who died four years previously. Angel asks Enrique to read his film script, entitled *The Visit*.

The plot of this script activates the second timeline. In 1977 the transvestite Zahara (i.e. Juan/Ignacio/Angel) visits the school where her brother, the real Ignacio, boarded as a boy with his classmate Enrique. In order to blackmail its director, Fr. Manolo (Daniel Gimenez Cacho), she shows him the story written by her brother, denouncing the abuse he suffered at the hands of the priest.

The reading of this text opens up the third timeline. In 1964 the young Ignacio makes friends with his classmate Enrique, and endures Fr. Manolo's insistent harassment.

In the initial part of this film the story twists upon itself, causing the audience to lose any sense of the passing of time. The characters get confused with each other, to the point where it is difficult to understand what has really happened and what belongs to realm of make-believe. Where is the truth? In 1980, in 1977, or in 1964? We will never know.

All the characters are divided between different lives, different stories, different faces. This laceration is concretely expressed in the image of Ignacio, as a child, falling and hurting his head while being chased by Fr. Manolo, during a trip to the countryside. Almodovar uses the rivulet of blood running down the child's face to tear the image from top to bottom. From that moment onwards, Ignacio is aware of his ambiguity. "A rivulet of blood divided my forehead in two, and I had a feeling that the same would happen with my life: it would always be divided, and I'd never be able to do anything to prevent that."

Volver (2006). In a town of the Mancha region – Almodovar's region of origin – women carefully clean the tombstones in a cemetery. A wide shot from right to left shows their work in detail and, at the same time, sets out the film's theme, which consists in illustrating the relationship between the living and the dead as it was experienced until recently – and is still experienced, at least in part – in rural Spain.

Two sisters, Raimunda (Penelope Cruz) and Soledad, known as Sole (Lola Duenas), together with Paula (Yohana Cobo), Raimunda's daughter, travel from Madrid to their native village to visit their elderly aunt Paula (Chus Lampreave). The latter is the sister of their mother and grandmother, who is believed to be dead, but in fact is not.

In Madrid, Sole works from home as a hairdresser. Raimunda works wherever she can as a cleaner. She has a good-for-nothing husband, Paco (Antonio de Torres), who attempts to assault Paula while his wife is away. Paula, having grabbed a kitchen knife, kills him almost without realizing it. Paco is not Paula's real father. Raimunda had become pregnant by her father before meeting her future husband, and Paco had agreed to assume paternity for the child.

The film proceeds with a series of complications. First of all, Raimunda needs to hide Paco's body. Meanwhile, she is left in charge of a closed restaurant, during a brief absence of its owner. A cinema troupe working nearby asks for refreshments, and the enterprising Raimunda prepares delicious meals for some thirty people, including their final dinner.

Back in the village, aunt Paula dies. Neither Raimunda nor the young Paula can attend her solemn funeral, because they are occupied with other business. Sole attends and, without realizing it, brings her elderly mother Irene (Carmen Maura) back to Madrid in the trunk of her car. Irene is believed to be dead, whereas in fact she was hiding in her sister's home and looking after her during her final illness.

Henceforth, Irene will wander amongst the living as if she were a ghost. Agustina (Blanca Portillo), a family friend who is suffering from a terminal illness, wants to know from the ghost whether her mother, who disappeared without trace, is dead or alive. Following the thread of this request, little by little we discover the family's dark secrets, which the dead had taken with them to their graves, and which are brought back to life by the living, who establish a relationship with the dead which will last as long as their memory lasts.

Game of mirrors

Broken Embraces (*Los abrazos rotos*, 2009). Cinematography, as an audiovisual technique, is considered an extension of sight and sound. But our senses can mislead us. Skillfully used, the technical perfection of cinematography can be a game changer: it can make what is false appear true, or make the truth appear false. We have already seen in his other films how Almodovar loves to play on different levels, creating in the cinema what cannot be found in real life, rendering visible what is invisible in reality – finding in the cinema the flip side of reality, which is to say the irrefutable proof of reality's ambiguity.

Mateo (Lluis Homar), a cinema director always on the look-out for an opportunity to make money, is in love with the beautiful Lena (Penelope Cruz), who passionately loves him back. But Lena is with Ernesto (Jose Luis Gomez), a wealthy industrialist of unlimited resources. Ernesto loves Lena with a possessive and destructive love which, naturally, is not returned.

Mateo makes Lena the star of the film he is directing. To prevent his woman being lured away, Ernesto becomes the producer (i.e. the owner) of the film, and puts his son, also named Ernesto (Ruben Ochandiano), in charge of filming work backstage. Using the material filmed by his son, Ernesto senior is able to decipher the secrets which Lena and Mateo exchange on set, with the help of an expert lip-reader (Lola Duenas). Thus he finds out that his woman not only does not love him, but actually hates him.

A film (the backstage takes) about a film (Mateo's) within a third film (Almodovar's), in which the director plays on the relationship between sound and image (the lip movements that require an expert's intervention to be interpreted...). The tangle is such that a dedicated student of communication sciences might go crazy with joy.

Lena notices that Ernesto junior is spying on her on his father's behalf. Having unsuccessfully attempted to rip the camera from him, she speaks directly into the lens and, from the screen, tells Ernesto senior what she thinks of him.

Lena appears in the room where Ernesto is watching his son's filming. "Focus on me!" Now she is doing her own voice-over of the silent film. Alternated on-screen we see close-ups of her acting mutely, with her own voice overlaid, and close-ups of her speaking aloud. An admirable game of mirrors between the reality "stolen" from cinema and the fiction which destroys an apparent reality, in search of the true one.

Another exciting moment comes when Lena and Mateo, conscious of the precariousness of their condition as clandestine lovers, are watching on television a sequence from the film *Journey to Italy,* by Rossellini. The sequence is the one where a couple in crisis (played by George Sanders and Ingrid Bergman) are present at the finding, amongst the ruins of Pompeii, of a plaster cast of the bodies of a married couple, who died in each other's embrace during the eruption of Vesuvius. Lena, seeing their embrace rendered eternal by the lava, tells Mateo that she, too, wants to die like that. Mateo takes his camera and, using its self-timer, takes a picture of himself embracing Lena. Will this be their eternity?

The Skin I Live In (*La piel que habito*, 2011). Doctor Ledgard (Antonio Banderas), an esteemed plastic surgeon, is a man of power, confident and determined. Heir to the mad scientist who often appears in horror films, Ledgard is a witch-doctor who pushes the boundaries of science in the depths of his laboratory. Consequently, he decides to ignore the ethics of medicine in pursuit of a terrible personal vendetta.

Almodovar's discourse on the transience of identity and the metamorphosis of bodies is tied in this film to a conversation about power, control and abuse.

During a rather wild party, the young Vicente (Jan Cornet) attempts to assault Norma (Blanca Suarez), Ledgard's underage daughter, who is traumatized and kills herself. Hence the vendetta of her father, who captures Vicente and, using advanced scientific procedures bordering on science fiction, transforms him into a girl whom he names Vera (Elena Anaya), and to whom he gives the features of his wife, who also committed suicide.

The relationship of submission and sadism established between the doctor and his victim, held in a luxurious villa, undergoes a transformation, however, as the budding Pygmalion falls in love with his creation.

The film moves between reality and dream in the dark atmosphere of a thriller, entwining various flashbacks. A real descent into the hell of the mind of this scientist, who re-lives the finding of his daughter's violated body in a forest worthy of a horror tale.

The menacing atmosphere of the forest contrasts, in another flashback, with the ascetic and excessively illuminated atmosphere of the operating theatre, where Vicente is transformed from a young man devoted to drugs and predatory sex into the masterpiece of the scientist-turned-artist.

The love he feels for Vera is not lucky for Ledgard. The girl – once a boy – takes advantage of his love to regain her freedom, although, from now onwards, she will have to be content with living in a skin which is not her own.

On Noah's ark

It is time to return to *Julieta*. We had left the woman, disconsolate, watching young girls play basketball. A second casual encounter with Bea brings more news of her daughter Antia, who lives in Switzerland with her family, and has found out that her mother still lives in their old apartment in Madrid.

Ava, her sculptor friend, who is afflicted by a terminal illness, informs Julieta of the obstructive role played by Marian (Rossy de Palma), Xoan's housekeeper, secretly in love with her boss and jealous of his new wife, who had sowed discord between mother and daughter.

In the end, Julieta receives a letter from Antia, who writes that the eldest of her three children, a nine-year-old boy, lost his life while swimming in a stream. Wracked with suffering, Antia understands the pain she herself inflicted on her mother when she left her without a word.

Julieta leaves immediately for Switzerland. To Lorenzo, who drives her in the car, she says: "I won't ask any questions. I won't say anything. I'll only try to be there for her, if she lets me…" "She's the one who included her address in the letter," says Lorenzo.

Thus, ends Almodovar's latest film. A glimmer of light opens up in the life of a woman who, because of her sinister fate, had become a prisoner to the judgements made of her, which were never rendered explicit in words, but expressed in the enigmatic, severe looks of people who misread her actions, attributing intentions which never crossed her mind.

This rapid digression through Almodovar's cinematography does not end with his latest film, but with a step back to his penultimate film, *I'm So Excited* (*Los amantes pasajeros*, 2013). A simple accident caused by two airport workers in Madrid produces a breakdown in the undercarriage of an airplane on its way to Mexico City. Suspended in the sky above Toledo, waiting to return to their starting point, passengers and crew meet and confront each other, entwining their destinies. In order to calm everyone down, the stewards and hostesses mix sleeping pills and some drugs into the drinks they serve to their passengers, who fall asleep.

All sorts of different characters are on this airplane: Norma (Cecilia Roth), a bondage teacher, who is in danger because an assassin hired to kill her is on the same flight; Bruna (Lola Duenas), a soothsayer anxious to lose her virginity; Ricardo (Guillermo Toledo), a *telenovelas* star, who continues to communicate with land via calls to his exes; Mr. Mas (Jose Luis Torrijo), a banker on the run from a series of illegal financial operations; a couple of newlywed drug addicts on their honeymoon (Miguel Angel Silvestre and Laya Marti).

Time passes, and all sorts of things happen on the airplane. Having used up its emergency fuel, the plane lands at the same airport from which it had departed. Nothing has happened. But the momentary release from inhibition, under the effect of sleeping pills and drugs, ensures that something has changed in the life of every survivor.

The airplane in *I'm So Excited* is like a metaphorical Noah's ark, welcoming a sample of the disparate cases which Almodovar has described in his films, painting them in grotesque colors, but without neglecting the sense of life's tragedy hiding behind each one.

On this airplane there might be a place for the unbalanced heroes of the *movida* in *Labyrinth of Passion*, the nuns in *Dark Habits*, with their spoiled tiger cub, the tragic lovers in *Law of Desire,* the eccentric *Women on the Verge of a Nervous Breakdown*; a place for Leo, lost in the city, and her mother, the lover of fresh country air, in *The flower of my Secret*, for the devoted friends in *All About my Mother*, the women in a coma in *Talk to Her*, the abused boarding school students in *Bad Education*, the ghosts in *Volver*, the lovers seeking immortality amongst the ruins of Pompeii in *Broken Embraces*, the crazy scientist and his victims in *The skin I Live In*, and of course for Julieta and Antia, mother and daughter finally reunited.

www.ingramcontent.com/pod-product-compliance
Lightning Source LLC
Chambersburg PA
CBHW071009160426
43193CB00012B/1976